MONETIZE YOUR LIST

The 90-day game plan to automate sales with your email list as a writer, coach, teacher, or speaker

Jonathan Milligan

PGB
PLATFORM GROWTH BOOKS

Book Cover by Platform Growth Books

Illustrations by Jonathan Milligan

1st edition 2025

YOUR FREE GIFT

As a way of saying thanks for your purchase, we are offering a free companion online course called, *The Monetize Your List Accelerator Course.*

With this companion online course, you'll be able to fully implement all the exercises, worksheets, and checklists inside this book. To get free instant access, go to:

MarketYourMessage.com/monetize-course

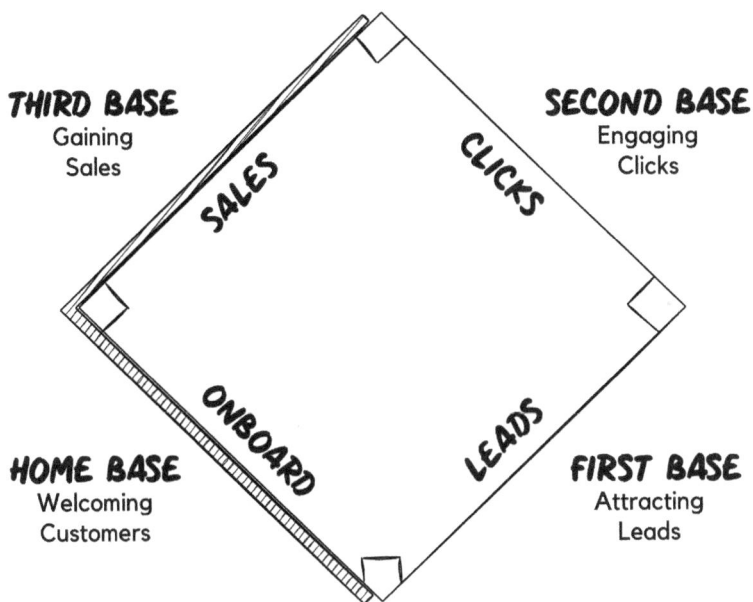

THIRD BASE
Gaining
Sales

SECOND BASE
Engaging
Clicks

SALES

CLICKS

ONBOARD

LEADS

HOME BASE
Welcoming
Customers

FIRST BASE
Attracting
Leads

The Diamond Customer Journey Map

Inside the pages of this book, you'll discover the Diamond Customer Journey Map. To monetize your list, you need to move people from lead (first base), to click (second base), to sale (third base), and to onboard (home base).

Contents

Introduction

The money is **not** in the list.

You've heard the gurus say it a thousand times: *"The money is in the list."* They make it sound easy. Just collect enough emails, and you'll have a six-figure business overnight. But if that were true, why do so many people build an email list only to struggle with low open rates, poor engagement, and disappointing sales?

Here's the truth: **The money is in the relationship.**

Your email list isn't a magic ATM. It doesn't print money just because people signed up. Before your list can generate sales, you need to build **authority, influence, and trust.** People buy from those they respect, learn from, and feel connected to. If your subscribers don't trust you, they won't buy from you—no matter how many emails you send.

Maybe you've experienced this yourself. You worked hard to grow your list. You sent emails promoting your product. But, you got zero engagement. You second-guess everything. *Did I say the wrong thing? Do people even want what I'm offering? Am I just bad at this?*

I get it. When I first started, I thought growing my list was the hard part. I chased bigger subscriber numbers. I thought sales would come in once I hit a certain threshold. But when the time came to sell, I was met with silence. **I had subscribers, but I didn't have relationships.**

That's when everything changed. I stopped focusing on numbers and started focusing on **connection.** I learned to write emails that felt like personal conversations, not marketing blasts. I built trust before asking for a sale. And I developed a **repeatable system** that turned casual subscribers into loyal customers.

Imagine this:

- Instead of struggling to sell, your emails naturally guide people toward buying.

- Instead of feeling like no one is listening, your subscribers eagerly open, click, and reply.

- Instead of unpredictable income, you have a **system that brings in sales automatically**—even while you sleep.

This book is going to show you how to make that happen.

The Diamond Customer Journey Map is key to this strategy. It's a simple, step-by-step framework. It moves people from subscriber to customer without being pushy or overly promotional. It's based on engagement, trust, and automation. No hype, no gimmicks—just a **proven process** to turn your list into a revenue-generating asset.

I know this works because I've **lived it.** I've seen it transform struggling email lists into thriving businesses. And now, I'm going to walk you through it step by step.

This book is for you if you're a writer, coach, speaker, or entrepreneur. It will help you monetize your email list. You won't annoy your audience or feel like a used car salesman.

Your list isn't just a collection of emails. It's a community. A business asset. A **bridge between where you are now and the success you want.**

And by the time you finish this book, you'll know exactly how to use it.

Are you ready? Let's dive in.

1

Why Your List Isn't Making Sales

In a small coastal village, there lived a fisherman named Akira. Every day, he would cast his net into the same spot, hoping for a bountiful catch. For weeks, he hauled in fish after fish, and his success became the talk of the town.

Emboldened by his good fortune, Akira decided to maximize his profits. He began casting his net more, sometimes hourly. He believed more attempts would yield more fish. But soon, the fish grew wary of the constant disturbance. They learned to avoid Akira's favorite spot. His once-bountiful catches dwindled to nothing.

Desperate, Akira sought advice from the village elder. The wise old man smiled and said, "Akira, you've forgotten the rhythm of the sea. The fish need time to gather and grow comfortable. Your impatience has driven them away. Give the waters rest, and they will reward you once again."

This parable shows a mistake many email marketers make. They bombard their lists with constant promotions. This drives away subscribers instead of nurturing relationships. In this chapter, we will help you build or rebuild trust with your email list.

The Mistakes That Break Trust

Sending emails sporadically is where many people stumble. You might send a flurry of emails for a week or two, then nothing for months. Life gets busy, you're unsure of what to say, or you're afraid of annoying subscribers with too many emails. So you just don't send anything at all.

Others swing to the opposite extreme. Every email is a pitch. Another sale, another product, another limited-time offer. Week after week, it's one promotion after another. This happens even with big-name experts. It's like being on a friend's text list where every message asks for money.

Some people take an even more hands-off approach. They only send something when they're launching a product. The rest of the time, their list is an afterthought.

Why Your Emails Aren't Connecting

Sporadic emails kill momentum. Think about a friend you only hear from once a year. When they finally text, it feels awkward. You don't know where the relationship stands. That's what it feels like when you don't email your subscribers regularly.

Constant promotions burn people out. Imagine a store where the salesperson follows you, pitching every five minutes. Eventually, you'd leave—and probably never come back. That's how relentless sales emails feel to your audience.

Neglecting your list altogether is like planting a garden and never watering it. By the time you need the flowers, they're wilted. If you ignore your email list, subscribers forget you. And when you suddenly reappear asking for something, they're less likely to respond.

Without consistent, meaningful interaction, your list stops being an asset. It becomes just a collection of email addresses. The trust, engagement, and loyalty that drive sales? All of that fades away.

How to Build a Connection That Lasts

Your email list isn't just a collection of addresses. It's a relationship—a living, breathing connection with real people. Like any meaningful relationship, it thrives on effort, trust, and care.

Start by seeing your subscribers as individuals, not potential customers. What would you do when building a friendship? You'd begin with a conversation. Share a story that makes them smile, or ask a question that sparks their curiosity. You wouldn't lead with a request; you'd start by offering something of value.

Find common ground. Pay attention to what resonates with your audience. Their clicks, replies, and engagement are clues. Maybe they're drawn to tips about productivity, inspiring personal stories, or practical advice on a shared challenge. Once you find those shared interests, lean into them. Build your conversations around what matters most to them.

Show up consistently. Relationships falter when you disappear. Your subscribers need to hear from you regularly, not just when you're launching something. And every time you show up, bring something valuable. Share a quick story, a surprising insight, or a practical takeaway. Something that makes them look forward to your emails, not dread them.

Engagement is the heartbeat of your list. Before you think about selling, think about connection. Spark curiosity. Get them clicking, replying, and nodding along as they read. If you nurture that engagement, you'll build a foundation of trust. And when the time comes to offer something, they'll be ready to listen—not because you pushed, but because you cared.

7 Keys to Building a Stronger Relationship with Your List

Building stronger relationships with your email list doesn't have to feel complicated. It's about approaching your audience as you would a new friend. Be genuinely interested, curious, and caring. When your emails feel like a chat with a good friend, your subscribers will feel more connected to you and your message.

Treat Emails Like Conversations

Emails should feel like a friendly chat, not a one-sided sales pitch. Imagine if the only time a friend called was to ask for something—how would that feel? Your emails should offer value, spark interest, or share a relatable story. Prioritize connection over conversion, and your readers will stick around longer. Don't worry if you are not sure how to do this. In a future chapter, I will share a game-changing formula you can use. Once you learn it, you will never struggle again with what to send to your email list.

Find Shared Interests

Your audience gives you clues every time they open, click, or reply. Pay attention. If they're clicking on productivity tips, they're telling you what they care about. Use this insight to craft emails that speak to their passions. The more your emails align with their interests, the deeper the connection becomes.

Nurture Before Selling

Trust isn't built overnight, and it's certainly not built by constantly pitching. Instead, show up with content that entertains, inspires, or solves a problem. Think of it like watering a plant—consistent care helps it grow. Once trust is established, your audience will be far more open to hearing about what you're offering.

Think Deposits, Not Withdrawals

Every email should feel like a gift. Your content should give your audience a sense of gain. It could be a practical tip, an inspiring story, or a thought-provoking question. If every email is an ask—buy this, sign up for that—your subscribers will quickly lose interest. Balance giving and asking to keep the relationship healthy.

Prioritize Consistency Over Perfection

The perfect email doesn't exist. What matters is showing up. Even if your email isn't perfectly polished, your consistency builds trust. Subscribers notice when you're reliable, and that reliability speaks volumes. Don't let perfectionism stop you from hitting "send."

Engage, Don't Just Inform

Think of your emails as the start of a dialogue. Ask questions, encourage replies, and let your audience know you're listening. Engagement builds community, and community builds loyalty. When subscribers feel heard, they're more likely to stay engaged.

Segment and Personalize

One-size-fits-all emails don't cut it anymore. Use what you know about your audience—whether it's their clicks, purchases, or replies—to create content that feels tailored to them. When your emails feel personal, subscribers are more likely to open, read, and trust what you send.

By focusing on these principles, you'll turn your email list into more than just a marketing tool. It'll become a community of loyal subscribers who trust you and are eager to hear from you.

Practical Exercise: Rebuilding Your Relationship with Your Email List

This exercise will help you evaluate your current approach and create a plan for stronger, more engaging emails. Follow these steps to find gaps. Then, refocus your strategy. Prioritize building relationships over making sales.

- **Step 1: Open Your Email Platform:** Locate the last 10 emails you sent to your subscribers.

- **Step 2: Label Each Email:** For each email, determine whether it's promotional or relational.

- **Step 3: Count the Balance:** Tally up how many emails were focused on selling versus providing value.

- **Step 4: Reflect on Your Approach:** Assess the balance of your emails. Are you consistently nurturing your list, or is it dominated by promotions?

Key Takeaways:

- Your email list is a relationship, not a transactional tool.

- Consistent value builds trust, which naturally leads to sales.

- Engage your subscribers through stories, shared interests, and meaningful dialogue.

2

The Diamond Customer Journey Map Explained

O ne of the best memories of childhood is the sound of a metal bat connecting with a baseball. Little League was the highlight of every spring. If you've ever been to a t-ball game, though, you know it's a little chaotic. The ball sits on a tee, the perfect target, and the kids take a swing. That's when the real entertainment begins.

One kid smacks the ball and runs straight to third base. Another sprints into the outfield, chasing butterflies instead of rounding the bases. Some kids freeze, stunned by the fact that they hit the ball. It's both adorable and frustrating. The chaos keeps the parents chuckling.

The whole point of t-ball isn't just to hit the ball; it's to learn the rules of the game. Once you know the rules, the chaos fades. Suddenly, there's a purpose in every play. That's how you win.

Email marketing works the same way. Without knowing the rules, it feels like t-ball. You're swinging wildly, hoping to connect but unsure of where to run once you do. For authors, coaches, and speakers, building an email list often feels just as chaotic. What do you say? How often do you email? What if people unsubscribe?

Understanding the rules changes everything. A strategy like the Diamond Customer Journey Map makes email marketing less overwhelming. Instead, it is a simple plan. It aims to build relationships, boost engagement, and see results. When you know the rules, you can finally step up to the plate with confidence and hit it out of the park.

Why Most Email Strategies Strike Out

Email marketing often feels like standing at home plate, unsure of where to swing. Many people freeze under the pressure of emailing their list. The fear of saying the wrong thing can feel crushing. What if subscribers leave? What if you lose more than you gain? It's paralyzing.

For others, it's the sheer complexity that stops them. Email marketing can seem like an endless maze of templates, tools, and tech jargon. The frustration builds until it feels easier to just avoid the whole thing.

When people do hit "send," they often default to broadcasting. They treat email like a megaphone, shouting their message to a faceless crowd. It's a one-way street—impersonal, detached, and uninspiring. There's no connection, no conversation, no real relationship.

It's no surprise this approach rarely works. Emails that feel like ads get ignored. Messages sent with no clear purpose fall flat. When communication is one-sided, subscribers stop listening. It's like trying to win a baseball game by throwing the ball into the stands—there's no chance of a home run.

Why the Broadcast Approach Falls Flat

The broadcasting approach might seem like the easiest way to reach your audience, but it's a swing and a miss. Blasting out one-size-fits-all messages often leads to low engagement. People skim, delete, or even unsubscribe. When emails feel generic or self-serving, readers tune out.

More importantly, it's a missed opportunity. Every email is a chance to build trust and connect. It shows your audience that you understand them. When emails are impersonal, that chance slips away. Instead of creating loyal fans, you're left with a disengaged list.

Broadcasting also sends the wrong message. It feels transactional as if all you care about is making a sale. No one wants to feel like just another number in a crowd. Relationships aren't built through a megaphone. Without a personal touch, your emails become noise in an already noisy inbox.

Breaking Down the Diamond Customer Journey Map

Email marketing isn't about swinging for the fences with every message. It's about guiding your subscribers step by step, just like running the bases in baseball. Each base is a key milestone, guiding your audience from curious onlookers to loyal customers. Let's break down the process step by step.

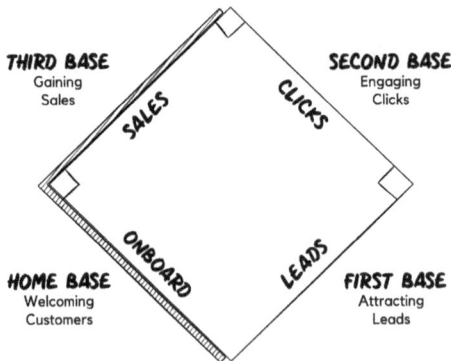

THIRD BASE
Gaining
Sales

SECOND BASE
Engaging
Clicks

SALES

CLICKS

ONBOARD

LEADS

HOME BASE
Welcoming
Customers

FIRST BASE
Attracting
Leads

First Base – Attracting Leads

The first step in any winning strategy is getting on base. In email marketing, that means attracting leads and building your list. You can't nurture relationships or make sales until people join your email community.

Owning your list is essential. Social media may seem the easier way to reach an audience. But, they are unpredictable. Algorithms shift, accounts get suspended, and trends change overnight. What happens to your connections if the platform disappears? You're back to square one.

Email is different. It's stable, dependable, and yours to keep. When someone joins your list, you have a direct, unblocked line of communication. Think of it as your business's safety net. It's a durable asset you can rely on, no matter how the digital landscape changes.

Your email list isn't just a collection of addresses. It's your tribe. These are people who've raised their hands, said, "I'm interested," and given you permission to reach out. That's powerful. Be intentional in attracting leads. It will build a lasting business.

Second Base – Engaging Clicks

Reaching second base means turning curiosity into engagement. This step is about knowing your subscribers. What interests them? What do they care about? How can you serve them better? The more you know about your audience, the more personal and impactful your emails become.

Segmentation is the key. It's not as complicated as it sounds. At its core, it's simply grouping people based on what they've shown interest in. You're not guessing—you're letting their actions tell you what they want.

A "click magnet" is a simple way to do this. A lead magnet draws in new subscribers, but a click magnet gets those already on your list to engage. For example, you might send an email offering a free book-writing checklist. When someone clicks to download it, they've just raised their hand to say, "I'm interested in writing a book." Now you know exactly who to talk to about your book-writing course.

Understanding your audience before you pitch makes all the difference. It's like offering a cold drink to someone who's just come in from the heat—it's timely, relevant, and appreciated.

Third Base – Making Sales

Reaching third base is where interest turns into action. By this stage, your subscribers have shown you what they care about. They've clicked, engaged, and demonstrated their interest. Now it's time to offer them something that aligns perfectly with what they're already looking for.

This is where sales emails become highly effective. When you customize your message for their interests, it feels less like a pitch. Instead, it feels like a natural next step. Automation makes this process seamless. Set up an email sequence that nurtures their curiosity and presents your offer at the right time. These emails can show your product's value. They can solve the reader's problem.

Not everyone on your list is ready for this step, and that's okay. Avoid burning out your audience by pitching only to those who've expressed interest. Your list can keep getting valuable content until they're ready to proceed. Talking to the right person, at the right time, about the right thing turns sales from a pushy transaction into a welcome opportunity.

Home Base – Onboarding and Upselling

Home base is where the game is won. After a subscriber makes a purchase, your work isn't done. This is the moment to solidify trust, build loyalty, and set the stage for a lasting relationship.

Onboarding is critical. A smooth, welcoming experience reassures your customers they've made the right choice. It helps them understand how to use your product, see its value, and feel confident in their decision. Good onboarding reduces refunds. It also creates happy, loyal customers. They stick around.

But don't stop there. Home base is also where you can guide customers toward higher-tier offers. Many buyers are eager to deepen their investment if you give them the chance. As one principle wisely puts it, "Some buyers will buy more if you make it available to them."

Upselling isn't about pressure; it's about meeting your customers where they are. Always offer the next step. It could be an upsell now or a chance to upgrade later. By doing so, you're helping them grow while creating a win-win for your business.

Don't worry if you're not sure how to implement this strategy. The rest of the book is designed to hold your hand and guide you one step (or base) at a time.

Personal Exercise: Map Your Momentum Exercise

Take a moment to grab a blank sheet of paper and a pen. Draw a simple baseball diamond in the center of the page.

Label the bases:

- First (Attracting Leads)

- Second (Engaging Clicks)

- Third (Making Sales)

- and Home (Onboarding and Upselling).

This will serve as a visual representation of your email marketing strategy.

Now, reflect on how you currently engage with your email list. What are you doing at each base?

- Start with First Base: Are you consistently attracting new leads to your list?

- Move to Second Base: Do you have a way to engage your subscribers and identify their interests?

- On Third Base, think about your sales strategy—are you making relevant offers at the right time?

- Finally, check Home Base. Are you onboarding customers and giving them chances to take the next step?

As you consider each base, ask yourself if there are any gaps or areas where you're losing momentum. Are you stuck at First Base because you're not actively building your list? Are you failing to advance to Home Base because your onboarding process is unclear? Jot down your observations next to each base on your map. This exercise shows you where to focus your efforts. It will help you improve your Diamond Customer Journey Map.

Key Takeaways:

- To connect with your email subscribers, know their journey from lead to loyal customer.

- Following the Diamond Customer Journey Map, step by step, builds stronger bonds and yields better results.

- Your email list is a valuable business asset. It won't be lost to changing algorithms or platforms.

3

Overcoming Common Email Marketing Challenges

E mail marketing is a powerhouse. For every dollar spent, it returns an average of $42. That's a staggering ROI—one that makes it hard to ignore. But here's the catch: 60% of marketers struggle to get their emails noticed. They pour their time and creativity into crafting messages that never truly connect.

The disconnect is frustrating. You know email marketing has the potential to transform your business. But how do you bridge the gap between what it *could* do and what it's actually doing for you?

This chapter dives straight into the heart of that question. It's about finding the common challenges in email marketing and, more importantly, how to overcome them. It's tough to find the right email frequency. Writing catchy subject lines and engaging content is hard, too. But the solutions are simpler than you might think.

The goal here is to move from potential to performance. By the end of this chapter, you'll know how to improve your emails. You'll make them connect better and get the results you've missed. Let's start closing the gap.

Turn Chaos into Connection: Email Strategy Reset

What if email marketing didn't feel like a guessing game? Imagine knowing exactly when to send, what to say, and how to keep your audience engaged. That's the power of doing things differently. It's about shifting from a scattershot approach to one that's intentional and reliable.

Start with consistency. People are creatures of habit, and your emails should be, too. A predictable schedule builds anticipation. It's the difference between being a welcome guest in someone's inbox or an unwelcome interruption.

Trust isn't built by selling. It's built by sharing stories, offering insights, and delivering value. Think of your emails as a way to start a conversation, not close a deal. When you show your audience you care and share relatable stories, they're more likely to stay and engage.

Not everyone on your list is the same. That's where segmentation comes in. Personalization isn't just using someone's name; it's speaking to their specific needs and interests. Tools make this easier than ever. They help you deliver the right message to the right person at the right time.

Simpler is better. Each email should have one clear message and one clear call to action. Cramming too much into one email is like a menu with a hundred options. People are more likely to walk away than decide.

Numbers don't lie. Your analytics tell you what's working and what's not. Open rates, click-through rates, unsubscribes—they're your guideposts. Reviewing them regularly isn't about chasing perfection; it's about steady improvement.

When you put these principles into play, email marketing becomes less of a chore and more of an opportunity. It's not about reinventing the wheel. It's about steering it in the right direction.

The Email Check-Up: Diagnosing and Fixing Common Challenges

Email marketing comes with its own set of hurdles. To understand what holds people back, I surveyed them. I asked about the biggest challenges in emailing an audience. The responses revealed seven key struggles that almost everyone faces at some point. Each challenge has a simple solution, and we'll address them all step by step throughout this book.

Challenge 1. Finding the Right Frequency

One of the top frustrations was figuring out how often to email. Send too many emails, and you risk overwhelming your audience. Send too few, and they might forget about you entirely. Striking the right balance is tricky because there isn't a one-size-fits-all answer. The sweet spot depends on your audience, your content, and how consistently you can show up.

The key is to experiment. Start with a weekly or bi-weekly schedule and track how your audience responds. Look for patterns in open rates, clicks, and unsubscribes. Your analytics will reveal whether you're hitting the mark or need to adjust. Frequency isn't about perfection—it's about predictability. When your audience knows when to expect you, trust begins to build.

Challenge 2. Getting More Engagement

Another common challenge was the lack of engagement. Many people said they feel like they're talking to a wall. Emails go out, but replies, clicks, and interactions are few and far between. This can be discouraging. You are putting in effort to create what you think is valuable content.

Engagement doesn't happen by accident. It requires creating moments of interaction. Think about ways to invite your audience into the conversation. A simple poll, an intriguing question, or a request for feedback can spark replies. When you design your emails with interaction in mind, you're no longer just a sender—you're part of a dialogue.

Challenge 3. Crafting Compelling Subject Lines

Writing subject lines that get noticed was a top concern. With inboxes overflowing, it's hard to stand out. A subject line is like a handshake—it's your first impression. If it doesn't catch their attention, the rest of your email doesn't stand a chance.

The best subject lines are brief, clear, and create curiosity. They hint at what's inside without giving it all away. Tools like Subjectline.com can help you refine your approach, but the real magic comes from knowing your audience. What problems do they want solved? What questions keep them curious? Tap into those, and your emails will stand out.

Challenge 4. Staying Consistent

Consistency was one of the most common struggles. It's easy to start strong, but life and work often get in the way. Skipping emails here and there can quickly turn into long gaps in communication. When that happens, trust with your audience begins to erode.

The solution lies in planning. A simple content calendar can make all the difference. Schedule email writing on specific days. This keeps you consistent, even when busy. Consistency doesn't mean perfection. It means showing up often enough to stay relevant.

Challenge 5. Fighting Irrelevance

Another major concern was staying relevant to an audience's changing needs. It's frustrating to put effort into an email, only to feel like it didn't resonate. Over time, an irrelevant email strategy can lead to lower engagement and even unsubscribes.

Relevance isn't something you guess—it's something you discover. Surveys, feedback forms, and direct questions can help you know your audience's needs. By checking in and adjusting your content based on their input, you can ensure your emails meet their needs.

Challenge 6. Balancing Brevity and Value

Many respondents said they struggle to strike a balance between keeping emails short enough to read but long enough to provide value. It's a delicate dance. Too brief, and it feels superficial. Too long, and it gets skipped.

The solution lies in structure. Frameworks like "Problem-Solution-Benefit" help you focus on delivering a single, impactful takeaway. When every sentence serves a purpose, you don't need a lot of words to make a big impact. It's about quality, not quantity.

Challenge 7. Avoiding Overwhelm

Finally, overwhelm came up as a major challenge. Many people admitted that the hardest part of email marketing is just sitting down to do it. Overwhelm can stop you before you start. It may be due to a lack of focus, too many priorities, or not knowing where to begin.

Breaking the process into smaller steps can make all the difference. Brainstorm ideas one day, draft another, and refine later. When you stop expecting perfection in one sitting, the task becomes far less daunting. Progress is built on small, consistent steps.

Each of these challenges is solvable, and we'll explore the solutions in depth as we go. For now, consider which of these struggles resonates most with you. Once you know what's holding you back, you can begin to clear the path forward.

Practical Exercise: Diagnose Your Email Marketing Challenges

Let's start by figuring out where you're stuck. Below are the seven most common email marketing challenges revealed in the survey. Take a moment to reflect on each one and jot down your honest answers. This will show you where to improve. It will also help you get ready to use the solutions we'll discuss later.

1. **Finding the Right Frequency**

   - Do you have a regular schedule for sending emails?

   - Are you worried you're sending too many emails—or not enough?

2. **Getting More Engagement**

   - Are your emails getting clicks, replies, or other forms of interaction?

   - Do you invite your audience to engage with polls or questions?

3. **Crafting Compelling Subject Lines**

- Do your subject lines grab attention?

- Have you tested different approaches to see what works best?

4. Staying Consistent

- Are you sending emails regularly, or is there a pattern of starts and stops?

- Do you feel prepared to write and schedule emails ahead of time?

5. Fighting Irrelevance

- Do you feel confident your content resonates with your audience's current needs?

- Have you asked your audience directly what topics or issues they care about most?

6. Balancing Brevity and Value

- Are your emails concise yet impactful?

- Do you use a clear structure like "Problem-Solution-Benefit" to focus your message?

7. Avoiding Overwhelm

- Do you feel stuck when it's time to write emails?

- Have you broken down your email process into smaller, manageable steps?

Once you've answered these questions, take a step back and look at your responses. Which of these seven challenges feels most familiar?

Are there a few areas where you're excelling, or do all of them feel like a struggle right now?

We will explore each challenge in depth and tackle them one by one using the Diamond Customer Journey Map. This simple, powerful system will help you. It will create a clear path for your emails. It will turn challenges into opportunities and frustrations into wins. You'll have a process that makes email marketing a growth tool, not a chore.

Key Takeaways

- Effective email marketing rests on consistency and relevance. Trust starts with showing up regularly and delivering valuable content.

- Engagement doesn't happen by chance. It's created by intention. It needs interaction, personalized content, and clear, compelling messages.

- A clear structure and a simple strategy can make email marketing feel doable, not overwhelming.

4

Misconceptions About Email Marketing

"Email is dead." It's a phrase tossed around at conferences and in marketing blogs. Small business owners whisper it as they try to keep up with trends. Social media feels flashy. Influencers seem unstoppable. But here's the truth—email isn't just alive. It's thriving.

Over 4 billion people use email every single day. That's half the planet logging in, scrolling through, and clicking on messages. If email is dead, someone forgot to tell billions of inboxes.

Take a small eCommerce brand that once believed the myth. They relied on social media ads and influencer partnerships to push their products. When sales slumped, they assumed email was old news—an outdated relic of the early internet days. Desperate for results, they decided to give it a shot.

Instead of blasting generic promotions, they launched a strategic campaign. They started small. They sent personalized product recommendations, a welcome series for new subscribers, and exclusive discounts for loyal customers. It didn't take long to see the impact.

Within six months, email became their top revenue source. They tripled their income and discovered something surprising. Likes and shares felt good. But, email was where real connections—and conversions—happened.

So, why does email still deliver? Why does it work when everything else feels crowded and noisy? Maybe the question isn't whether email is dead. Maybe it's whether you're using it to its full potential.

Why the "One-Size-Fits-All" Approach Fails

You open your inbox and see a subject line screaming, "Big Sale! Don't Miss Out!" You click it out of curiosity, only to find a generic email filled with products you don't care about. Annoying, right? You delete it without a second thought—or worse, hit "unsubscribe."

This is the reality of "batch-and-blast" email marketing. It's the spray-and-pray approach. You send the same message to everyone on your list, hoping something sticks. There's no thought about who's receiving it, what they care about, or why they signed up in the first place.

In a world where every ad and post fights for attention, a generic email feels like noise. It's a waste of time for the recipient and a wasted opportunity for you.

The real problem? Treating your email list as a crowd instead of a group of individuals. It's like shouting into a room full of people, hoping the right person hears you. Instead, what if you could walk up to each person and share something they actually want to hear? That's the power of personalization and segmentation.

Most businesses skip this step. They don't bother sorting their subscribers by interest, behavior, or demographics. They ignore the data and treat their list as a monolith. But email isn't about reaching everyone. It's about connecting with the right ones.

The Price of Being Irrelevant

Imagine entering a bookstore. The clerk hands you a cookbook. You wanted a mystery novel. Frustrating, right? That's exactly how people feel when they open a generic email that has nothing to do with their interests or needs.

When emails miss the mark, engagement plummets. Open rates sink because the subject line doesn't grab attention. Click-through rates flatline because the content inside feels meaningless. It's not that people don't care about emails—it's that they don't care about emails that don't care about *them*.

Relevance is everything. People want to feel like the message was written with them in mind. Without that connection, your email is just digital clutter. And the worst part? Low engagement sends a message to email providers. Poor performance flags your emails as unimportant. They may end up in spam folders.

So, what's the result of a generic, one-size-fits-all approach? You don't just lose clicks and conversions. You lose trust. And once trust is gone, it's tough to win back. Email marketing isn't just about sending messages. It's about sending the *right* message to the *right* person at the *right* time. Without that, your efforts fall flat.

Building Trust One Opt-In at a Time

Nobody likes an uninvited guest. The same goes for email. Sending messages to people who didn't ask for them is like showing up to an uninvited party. It's awkward, unwelcome, and bound to fail.

The solution? Build a permission-based email list. It starts with genuine opt-ins. These people want to hear from you. They've shared their email because they think you have something valuable to offer.

Why does this matter? Because permission creates trust. When someone opts in, they're essentially saying, "I'm interested. Tell me more." That's your green light to start a relationship. Don't overwhelm them with hard sales or irrelevant content. Instead, deliver value.

Forget shortcuts like buying email lists. Sure, it might look like a fast track to a bigger audience, but it's a dead end. Purchased lists often cause low engagement and high unsubscribe rates. They may even lead to spam complaints. Instead, focus on earning every subscriber by offering something they truly care about.

Make your opt-in irresistible. It could be a guide, a discount, or a free workshop. When you focus on quality over quantity, your list is more than just a collection of emails. It becomes a community of people who trust you, value your message, and are ready to engage.

In the pages ahead, we will help you improve the ROI in your email marketing. But first, we must address some misconceptions. They keep people from fully committing to email marketing.

Why Email Marketing Delivers the Best ROI

Email marketing isn't just a tool—it's a powerhouse for growing your business. It beats other marketing methods in ROI, engagement, and results. Unlike flashy trends that come and go, email endures. It is a reliable and flexible strategy for decades.

So, what makes email marketing so effective? Here are seven key reasons why this channel remains a top choice for businesses, big and small.

Unmatched ROI

Email marketing is a budget-friendly powerhouse. For every $1 spent, businesses see an average return of $36. That's not just a good deal—it's an extraordinary one.

What makes the ROI so high? Email lets you reach your audience directly. It has no ad costs or algorithm risks. A timely email campaign can boost sales, retention, and loyalty. Unlike paid ads, you have to keep paying to stay visible. An email list is a one-time investment that keeps paying dividends.

Small businesses, in particular, benefit from email's cost-effectiveness. A single automated sequence, like a welcome series, can boost sales. It requires little ongoing effort. It's a strategy that works for tight budgets and ambitious growth goals alike.

Direct Access to Your Audience

When you send an email, it lands directly in your audience's inbox. No middleman, no guessing games. Unlike social media, where algorithms decide who sees your posts, email puts you in control.

This direct access ensures your message gets seen. Social platforms are noisy and competitive, with posts often buried in endless feeds. Email, on the other hand, offers a quiet, focused space where your audience is more likely to engage.

More importantly, you own your email list. Social media platforms can change their rules, but your email list is yours to keep. It's a long-term asset. It protects your connection with your audience, no matter what changes in the digital world.

Highly Personalizable and Targeted

Email marketing isn't one size fits all. Today's platforms let you segment your audience. You can then tailor messages to specific groups. This level of personalization turns a generic broadcast into a meaningful conversation.

Imagine a clothing store. It sends a winter coat promo to customers in snowy areas. It offers swimwear deals to those in sunny regions. By knowing your audience's preferences and behaviors, you can deliver relevant, timely content.

Personalization goes beyond names in subject lines. It's about showing your audience that you understand them. When your emails feel personal, engagement skyrockets. This boosts open rates, clicks, and, ultimately, sales.

Wide Audience Reach

Email is universal. With over 4 billion daily users worldwide, it's a platform that reaches almost everyone. No matter your audience's age, location, or interests, chances are they have an email address.

This wide reach makes email uniquely versatile. Email is a great way to reach busy professionals, stay-at-home parents, or college students. Also, email works for all ages and industries. Unlike newer platforms, they skew to specific demographics.

The numbers speak for themselves. As the number of email users continues to grow, so does the opportunity to expand your reach.

It's a channel that adapts as your audience grows, ensuring you're always where your customers are.

Mobile-Friendly Engagement

People check their email constantly—on the bus, at work, and even while standing in line at the coffee shop. More than 60% of emails are opened on mobile devices. This makes email marketing ideal for our busy, on-the-go lives.

This mobile dominance is a huge advantage. A simple, appealing email can reach someone during their morning commute or while they're scrolling in bed. Unlike lengthy blog posts or desktop-only platforms, email fits seamlessly into busy schedules.

To capitalize on this, it's crucial to design emails with mobile in mind. Think clean layouts, concise text, and buttons that are easy to tap. When your emails look great on any device, you're more likely to capture attention—and conversions.

Scalable for Any Business Size

Email marketing scales effortlessly. It works for both a one-person shop and a Fortune 500 company. Automated workflows, templates, and scheduling tools make it simple to manage campaigns, no matter your resources.

For small businesses, email is a game changer. You don't need a big budget or a marketing team to create impactful campaigns. A few, well-planned sequences can nurture leads. They can build relationships and drive sales, all on autopilot.

For bigger companies, email scalability stands out. It can manage complex campaigns easily. Email platforms can grow with your business. They can do advanced segmentation and multi-step automation. This keeps your marketing effective at any stage.

Measurable and Data-Driven

Email marketing doesn't leave you guessing. With detailed analytics, you can track your campaign. It covers open rates, click-throughs, and conversion rates.

This data is gold. It tells you what's working and what's not, so you can fine-tune your approach. If a subject line falls flat, you'll know. If a particular CTA drives results, you can double down. Every email sent is a chance to learn and improve.

Analytics also help you make informed decisions about your audience. Study behavior patterns to find what works. Then, tailor future campaigns. This feedback loop makes email a top marketing tool. It's both adaptable and efficient.

Email marketing isn't just effective—it's essential. Email has the best ROI. It also connects you directly with your audience. That's why it's the cornerstone of successful business strategies. When done right, email doesn't just deliver results. It transforms how you engage, connect, and grow.

Practical Exercise: Start with One Personalized Email

Here's a simple way to take action right now.

1. **Choose One Segment:** Pick a small group from your email list. If you don't have segments set up, start with people who recently signed up or made a purchase.

2. **Write a Helpful Email:** Create a short email that feels per-

sonal. Share a personal story and a lesson you learned.

3. **Add a Call-to-Action:** End the email with one clear action you'd like them to take. For example, "Click here to read more" or "Reply to this email with your thoughts."

4. **Send It:** Send the email and watch for engagement. Pay attention to how many people open it and click the link (most email platforms will show you this data).

This small step helps you practice personalization and see how your audience responds. It's quick, easy, and sets the foundation for more effective email marketing.

Key Takeaways

- Personalization is key to successful email marketing. Generic, mass emails lead to low engagement and wasted opportunities.

- A permission-based email list builds trust. It connects you with an audience that wants to hear from you.

- Email marketing has the highest ROI. It gives you direct access to your audience. It is scalable and provides insights through detailed analytics.

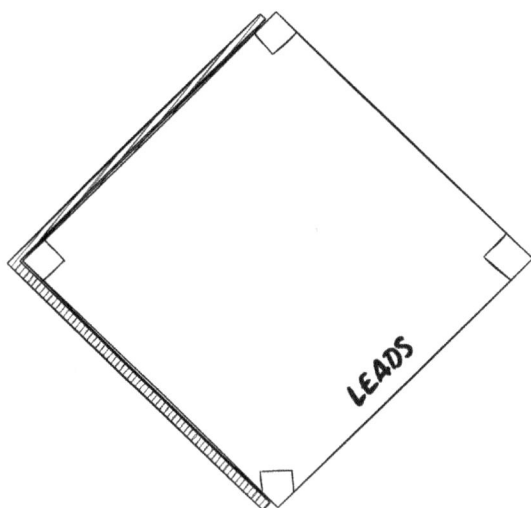

First Base:
Attracting Leads

5

First Base: Attracting Leads

I magine a busy travel site, LesFrenchies. It has many social media fans who love its content. They've got engagement—the likes, shares, and comments are rolling in. But there's a problem no one can see at first glance. Their posts aren't reaching as many people anymore. Algorithms, those unseen gatekeepers of social media, are tightening the rules. LesFrenchies is losing control over who sees its content.

They knew something had to change. So, they made a bold move. They stopped relying on social platforms. Instead, they offered free travel guides for email addresses. Next, they synced their Shopify store with GetResponse. This captured leads and created a direct line to their audience.

What happened next was remarkable. Their email open rates hit an impressive 50%, with click-through rates soaring to 4%. They transformed casual followers into a connected, engaged community they could reach on their terms.[1]

That's the power of attracting leads. Leads aren't just email addresses; they're the heartbeat of your business. They keep your message alive, fuel your growth, and open doors to new opportunities.

Let's explore why leads matter so much—and how to start bringing them into your world.

Chasing the Social Media Mirage

Social media feels like the easiest way to connect with an audience. It's flashy, it's immediate, and it's free—at least on the surface. But here's the catch: algorithms. Those unseen forces decide who gets to see your content and who doesn't.

Today, a post might reach thousands. Tomorrow, it could disappear into the void. The rules keep changing, and businesses scramble to keep up. The result? Dependence on paid ads to stay visible. What once felt like a free-flowing stream of opportunity now feels like a trickle.

The Problem With Vague Promises

A lot of businesses try to entice leads with generic offers. A PDF titled "5 Tips for Success," or an outdated checklist that doesn't address real needs. The problem isn't just that these lead magnets are boring—it's that they don't deliver value.

When someone takes the bait on a low-value offer, what happens next? They either unsubscribe or never engage. They realize it's not worth their time. Either way, it's a missed opportunity.

Algorithm Dependence

Social media platforms are not your business partners. They're businesses in their own right, and their loyalty lies with their bottom line. That's why they tweak algorithms to favor ads over organic content. They don't care about your reach—they care about their revenue.

You're on shaky ground if you rely solely on social media to connect with your audience. One algorithm update can cut your visibility in half overnight. You don't own your audience; the platform does.

The Missing Human Touch

Generic lead magnets might check a box, but they fail to spark a connection. People want to feel seen and understood. When your offer doesn't address a specific need or solve a real problem, it falls flat.

Think about it. If you offer nothing meaningful, why stay? This leads to high unsubscribe rates, low engagement, and a list that looks good on paper but is worthless.

To escape these traps, you need a new approach. It must put you in control and focus on providing real value to those you want to serve.

The Great Eight of Lead Generation

The race for followers is a losing game. Followers might like your content, but they don't give you control. They don't make your business sustainable. Email subscribers do.

By providing real value for an email address, you build relationships, not just a list of names. Relationships where you control the communication. No algorithms, no middlemen, just a direct line to the people who care about what you have to say.

This isn't about throwing together a quick freebie and hoping it sticks. It's about creating high-value, personalized incentives. They should excite people to join your list. The Great Eight is your blueprint for doing just that. Each method aims to give your audience what they want. It also reinforces your authority and expertise.

When you prioritize these meaningful exchanges, you're not just generating leads. You're creating a community of engaged subscribers who trust you and want to hear from you. This is how you build a system that works, no matter what changes in the social media landscape.

The shift is simple but profound. Stop chasing numbers and start offering value. The results will speak for themselves.

To reach first base in our Diamond Customer Journey Map, you must learn how to attract leads. Leads come before a relationship can be built, and a relationship comes before sales.

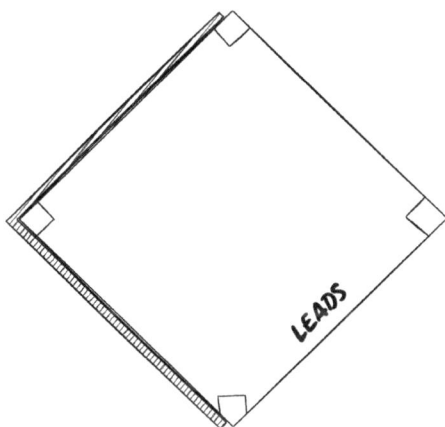

To grow your list fast, consider implementing these eight list-building strategies.

The Value Exchange: Making Every Email Count

When you ask someone for their email, you're asking for more than a few clicks—you're asking for trust. What is the best way to earn it? Give them something they can't wait to get their hands on.

A high-value PDF is one of the simplest yet most effective ways to do this. Think of it as a gift with a purpose. A checklist, a quick-start guide, or a usable resource. The key is tailoring it to solve a specific problem your audience has.

For example, a fitness coach might offer a "7-Day Meal Plan for Beginners." It's specific, actionable, and instantly valuable. Once they download it, they're engaged with your brand. You've gained a subscriber who's truly interested.

The Newsletter Tease: Creating Curiosity

Social media isn't just for likes; it's a powerful tool to drive email sign-ups. The trick is to tease the value your email list provides.

A post reads: "This week's newsletter shares my top three tools to double your productivity."" Want the list? Subscribe now!"

It's short, it's intriguing, and it hints at exclusive value. By previewing what subscribers can expect, you aren't just asking them to join. You're giving them a reason they can't ignore.

The Author Swap: Growing Together

You don't have to go it alone. Teaming up with others in your niche can help you reach more people and provide value to your audience.

The Author Swap is simple. You collaborate with a creator whose audience matches yours. You then exchange free digital resources like a book. They share your guide or eBook with their list, and you do the same with theirs.

It's a win-win. You both grow your lists, and your audiences benefit from fresh, relevant content. For example, a travel blogger might team up with a packing expert. They would exchange guides on travel hacks and packing tips. Book Funnel is an online software that makes it easy to set up these author swaps.

The Reader Magnet: Sweetening the Deal

When someone buys your book, they've already shown they're invested in your message. That's the perfect time to offer them a little something extra.

A reader magnet could be a free mini-course. It would dive deeper into your book's content. Or, it could be a bonus chapter that didn't make the final draft. It's a way to thank them for their purchase while bringing them into your email community.

For example, a personal finance book author could offer a free, downloadable budgeting template as a bonus. It's practical and relevant. It keeps readers engaged with your brand after they finish the last page.

Each strategy builds trust, adds value, and turns casual chats into real connections. It's not about the numbers—it's about the quality of the leads you attract and the relationships you build.

The 2-Step Post: Simple and Subtle

Social media posts grab attention. But, they often fail to drive action. The 2-Step Post changes that.

Here's how it works: you create a post promoting a valuable PDF—something your audience truly wants. Instead of cluttering the post with links, you place the download link in the first comment.

Why does this work? It feels less like a sales pitch and more like a conversation. The comment section becomes the bridge between interest and action. A productivity coach might post, "Want my free guide to beat procrastination?" Check the comments for the link!" It's simple, effective, and keeps the process friction-free.

The Self-Liquidating Offer: Leads That Pay for Themselves

A free physical book sounds expensive. But there's a catch: you ask the customer to cover the shipping cost. This strategy, known as a self-liquidating offer, does two things. First, it gets you a qualified lead. If someone's willing to pay shipping, they're serious about engaging with your content. Second, it offsets your expenses. So, it's a cost-neutral or even profitable lead generation tool.

Picture this: a business author offers a $20 book for free. Readers pay $7 for shipping. Not only does this cover printing and postage, but it also creates a win-win situation. Readers gain a resource. The author builds a list of leads primed for future offers.

On-Demand Video or Live Training: Value in Real Time

Nothing builds trust like teaching your audience directly. A free training video or webinar shows your skills and helps your audience with a real problem.

For example, a marketing expert might host a free live session on "How to Write Emails That Convert." During the registration process, attendees share their email addresses. You've delivered value and built your list. Your leads are now interested in your expertise.

The beauty of this approach is its flexibility. Record the session once. Use it as an on-demand resource. Or, host live events for real-time interaction. Either way, it's a powerful tool for attracting leads.

Quizzes: Engaging and Insightful

People love quizzes. They're fun, interactive, and offer instant feedback. More importantly, they're a goldmine for lead generation.

The secret lies in personalization. A health coach, for instance, could create a quiz titled "What's Your Energy Type?" Participants answer a few questions. They get results and enter their email to see a deeper analysis.

Quizzes work because they create curiosity. People want to learn more about themselves. They will trade their email for insights that feel special and personal.

These strategies go beyond the basics of lead generation. They focus on creating value, sparking interest, and building meaningful connections. It's not about chasing numbers—it's about building a list that works for you and your audience.

Practical Exercise: Crafting Your Lead Generation Strategy

This exercise will help you take action on the ideas in this chapter. Choose one of the Great Eight lead generation methods. Then, start building your system to attract leads. Follow these steps to get started:

1. Review the Great Eight: Reflect on the lead generation methods in this chapter. Which one stands out to you?

- The Value Exchange

- The Newsletter Tease

- The Author Swap

- The Reader Magnet

- The 2-Step Post

- The Self-Liquidating Offer

- On-Demand Video or Live Training

- Quizzes

2. **Choose Your First Strategy:** Pick one method that feels most practical for your audience and goals. Write it down.

3. **Define Your Value Offer:** What will you provide in exchange for an email address? Be specific.

   - If you chose The Value Exchange, describe the high-value PDF you'll create.

   - For The Newsletter Tease, outline the type of exclusive content you'll preview.

   - For Quizzes, decide on a theme that connects with your audience's interests.

4. **Set Up Your System:** Identify the tools you'll need to execute your strategy.

   - Landing page software, email marketing platform, or quiz builders.

   - Social media scheduling tools for methods like the 2-Step

Post or The Newsletter Tease.

5. **Create a Timeline:** Set a deadline for launching your lead generation strategy. Break it into smaller steps. First, create your resource. Next, set up your landing page. Finally, promote it on your chosen platform.

6. **Evaluate and Adjust:** Once your lead generation system is live, monitor your results. Track metrics like sign-ups, open rates, and engagement. Use this data to refine your approach and improve future efforts.

This step is not just theory; it's about using a tested strategy. It helps you create a sustainable email list that will grow your business.

Key Takeaways:

- Build an email list to own your audience. Don't rely on social media platforms you don't own.

- Attract high-quality leads by offering value for email addresses. This creates lasting connections.

- Use sustainable lead generation systems. They should deliver long-term results, not just quick wins.

6

Creating Irresistible Lead Magnets

Picture a farmer in the 1800s, flipping through the pages of a free almanac handed out by John Deere. Inside, he finds planting schedules, weather predictions, and advice for maximizing his harvest. It's not just helpful; it's indispensable. Every tip ties back to the tools John Deere sold. They showed farmers how these products could transform their fields.

This wasn't just an almanac. It was one of the first lead magnets. It was a tool to attract the right audience by offering something valuable. The farmers got useful insights. John Deere earned their trust, paving the way for future sales.[2]

Today, lead magnets are everywhere. They come in the form of free downloads, quizzes, or templates. Yet, most of them fail to capture attention, let alone build trust. Why? Because they miss the mark.

This chapter is all about creating lead magnets that people actually want. Not just for the sake of downloads, but to attract the right audience—the ones ready to take action. It's about leaving behind forgettable freebies. It's time to create something irresistible.

Where Most Lead Magnets Fall Short

Lead magnets are meant to attract and engage, but too often they miss the mark. Instead of creating excitement, they leave people unimpressed—or worse, uninterested. Here's where things go wrong:

Bland and Forgettable Content

Lead magnets with outdated PDFs or generic tips, like "Top 10 Marketing Secrets," fail. These uninspired offers lack originality and fail to stand out in a sea of similar content. They feel more like filler than value, leaving your audience asking, "What's in it for me?"

Trying to Be Everything to Everyone

When lead magnets try to cover too much, they lose focus. Broad topics like "The Complete Guide to Success" may seem ambitious. However, they often attract unqualified leads. These leads usually don't fit your business. By trying to appeal to everyone, you end up resonating with no one.

Too Much Information, Too Little Engagement

Dense eBooks or complex courses may look good, but they often confuse rather than assist. When a lead magnet feels like a mountain to climb, most people won't even start. The excitement of downloading it fades the moment they see how much effort it requires.

Weak Presentation and Messaging

A lead magnet's design and language say a lot about your brand. Poor visuals, cluttered layouts, and vague calls to action make your offer easy to dismiss. If your audience doesn't feel drawn in at first glance, they'll likely move on without giving it a second thought.

Lead magnets should create excitement, solve problems, and build trust. But when they're generic, overly complicated, or poorly executed, they fail to do any of those things. Instead of opening doors, they close them.

How to Create Lead Magnets That Work

Most lead magnets fail because they try to do too much or appeal to too many. To stand out, you need to create lead magnets that deliver value quickly and resonate deeply. Here's how to do it:

Solve One Specific Problem

Lead magnets work best if they fix one key problem. It should be something your audience wants to fix now. The key is specificity. Solving multiple problems or giving general advice will dilute your lead magnet. It will lose focus and impact. Instead, hone in on one challenge and provide a clear, actionable solution. A guide titled "Five Writing Prompts to Beat Writer's Block in 10 Minutes" speaks to their pain. It helps an audience with writer's block.

Specificity builds trust. It shows your audience that you understand their struggle and have a solution tailored to their needs. Think of it as a conversation starter. By solving one problem, you're opening the door to a deeper relationship where you can address more complex issues later.

Make It a Perfect Match for Your Offers

Your lead magnet should act as a bridge, seamlessly connecting your free content to your paid offers. If your lead magnet attracts the wrong audience, it won't matter how good your product is. Those leads won't convert. To avoid this, design your lead magnet as a natural extension of your main offer. If you sell a course on social media, a lead magnet like "The Ultimate Instagram Hashtag Template" is a perfect fit.

A strong link between your lead magnet and your offer is key. You're not just building a list. You're building a list of people interested in your product. This alignment also makes it easier to nurture leads, as the transition from free to paid feels natural and logical.

Deliver Value Instantly

The modern audience craves speed. They want solutions they can implement immediately without investing hours of their time. Lead magnets that offer quick wins are far more engaging than those that require a significant commitment. A checklist someone can use in five minutes or a template that solves an immediate problem feels like a gift rather than a task.

Instant value also builds momentum. When your audience experiences a small success because of your lead magnet, they're more likely to trust you and take the next step. Think of it as a taste test—they get a sample of your expertise and realize they want more. This is why offering actionable content that delivers results quickly is so powerful.

Appeal to the Eyes and Mind

The look of your lead magnet is just as important as the content inside. A cluttered or poorly designed lead magnet can mislead. It can make your audience doubt your brand's quality. On the other hand, a clean, visually appealing design creates an immediate sense of trust and professionalism. Use bold headlines, plenty of white space, and easy-to-read fonts to make your lead magnet inviting.

Design isn't just about aesthetics—it's about functionality. The layout should guide your audience through the content effortlessly. Think about the experience of using your lead magnet. Is the information easy to find? Does it flow logically? These small details make a big difference in whether your audience feels compelled to use what you've provided.

When done right, lead magnets become more than a freebie. They're a powerful tool for building trust, delivering value, and attracting the exact audience you want to serve.

Practical Exercise: Build Your Irresistible Lead Magnet

Creating a lead magnet that captures attention and delivers value doesn't have to be complicated. Follow these steps to craft a freebie your audience will love and use.

Step 1: Identify a Specific Pain Point

- Take a moment to brainstorm. Write down three common frustrations or challenges your target audience faces. These should be specific and highly relevant to their needs.

- Look at your list and circle the one pain point that feels the most urgent or universal. This will become the focus of your lead magnet. *Example*: If your audience consists of new entrepreneurs, one pain point could be, "I don't know how to create a business plan that's simple and actionable."

Step 2: Choose the Best Format

- Consider the problem you've chosen and ask: What's the easiest way to deliver a solution?

- Pick a format that is simple to create and quick for your audience to use. Some popular options are:

  - Checklists

  - Templates

  - Quizzes or assessments

  - Swipe files

  - Short videos or guides

- The goal is to make it feel like a quick win. *Example*: For the business plan challenge, you could create "The One-Page Business Plan Template."

Step 3: Draft the Content

- Begin drafting a solution to the problem, focusing on clarity and actionability.

- Make sure the content is concise and can be consumed in 5-10 minutes. Avoid overwhelming details—this is about giving your audience a taste of success.

- Include actionable instructions or fill-in-the-blank sections to simplify implementation. Example: In the business plan template, add sections with prompts like "Describe your target customer in one sentence" or "Name three main goals for the next 90 days."

Step 4: Design Your Lead Magnet

- Use a tool like Canva to create a visually appealing layout. Professional visuals build trust and make your lead magnet feel more valuable.

- Write a compelling headline that captures attention and clearly communicates the benefit.

- Include a strong call-to-action, such as "Download your free template and start seeing results today!"

- Use clean design principles: bold headers, plenty of white space, and easy-to-read fonts. *Example*: For the business plan template, you might use a clean, minimalist design with clear sections, bolded headers, and a downloadable PDF format.

Once you've completed these steps, test your lead magnet with a small group of your audience. Gather feedback, refine it, and get ready to watch it work its magic. With thoughtful planning and execution, you'll create a lead magnet that builds trust and attracts the right people to your offers.

Key Takeaways

- Focus on solving a specific problem to create lead magnets that resonate deeply with your audience.

- Design lead magnets that align seamlessly with your core offers to attract the right people.

- Make your lead magnets visually appealing, easy to consume, and instantly actionable.

7

The Power of Email Newsletters

J ustin Welsh started with a simple idea: a weekly email newsletter called *The Saturday Solopreneur*. Every Saturday, like clockwork, it landed in inboxes, delivering value-packed insights for solopreneurs. Within 12 months, over 77,000 people subscribed. That newsletter helped him build a $1.7 million solo business in just over three years.[3]

It wasn't flashy. No gimmicks, no overnight hacks. Just consistent, value-driven communication. Each week, Justin offered something his readers could use—advice, inspiration, clarity. And it worked. His story shows what's possible when you commit to a newsletter with purpose and care.

Imagine having a direct line to the people who want what you offer. A chance to show up in their lives regularly, build trust, and provide something they genuinely look forward to. That's the power of a weekly newsletter.

But here's the catch: most people get it wrong. It's easy to treat a newsletter like an afterthought or, worse, a sales pitch. Done that way, it's a waste of time for you and your audience.

This chapter is about getting it right. It's about creating a newsletter that your readers want to open, one that builds relationships and drives results. Not just clicks or opens but real, lasting impact for your business.

Let's figure out how to do it better.

Common Missteps That Undermine Your Newsletter

Sporadic emails don't build trust. They confuse your audience and make them question your reliability. When emails show up randomly, readers forget why they subscribed in the first place. A newsletter without consistency is like a café that's only open when the owner feels like it—people stop showing up.

Turning your newsletter into a sales pitch backfires. Readers didn't subscribe to be bombarded with promotions. They want value—insights, advice, or even a little inspiration. Constant selling feels transactional, not relational. It's like inviting someone to coffee and spending the entire time trying to sell them a product.

Subject lines that fail to spark curiosity get ignored. Your email is competing against dozens, maybe hundreds, of others in a crowded inbox. A bland or generic subject line is a surefire way to stay unopened. It's the digital equivalent of a door-to-door salesperson knocking half-heartedly and mumbling their pitch.

Content without a purpose leaves readers disengaged. People open your newsletter hoping for something useful, entertaining, or thought-provoking. When the email lacks direction or value, they're left wondering why they bothered. Confusion quickly turns into apathy, and apathy leads to unsubscribes.

Skipping teasers for future content is a missed opportunity. Anticipation is powerful. Readers are more likely to stick around if they know what's coming. Without a reason to stay engaged, they may not even realize what they're missing when they don't open your next email.

These mistakes may seem small, but they add up. A newsletter isn't just another task on your to-do list—it's a chance to connect and build trust. When approached carelessly, it becomes noise. When done well, it becomes your most valuable tool.

Why These Mistakes Hurt Your Newsletter

Inconsistency undermines credibility. When readers can't predict when—or if—they'll hear from you, they lose trust. A sporadic schedule signals disorganization and a lack of commitment. People want to engage with someone they can count on, not someone who shows up only when it's convenient.

Overloading with sales pitches pushes people away. Nobody enjoys being treated like a walking wallet. When your emails are all about you—your products, your offers, your agenda—readers disengage. Loyalty evaporates when value is replaced with constant self-promotion.

Weak subject lines leave your emails invisible. Even the most thoughtfully crafted newsletter goes unread if the subject line doesn't spark curiosity. An uninspired subject is like a blank billboard on a busy highway—nobody stops to look.

Unfocused content creates confusion. Readers open your emails expecting clarity and value. When they're met with scattered ideas or irrelevant information, they stop paying attention. A newsletter that feels directionless sends a message: you don't know what you're offering, so why should they care?

Failing to build anticipation is a missed chance to hook your audience. Teasers aren't just about marketing—they're about creating excitement and curiosity. Without them, your newsletter becomes just another email in an already crowded inbox.

How to Rethink Your Newsletter

Start treating your newsletter like a signature product. It's not just another task or a box to check—it's a cornerstone of your brand. When approached thoughtfully, a newsletter becomes more than an email. It becomes an experience.

Think of it as an extension of your mission and personality. Everything from the subject line to the content should reflect who you are and what your business stands for. It's your opportunity to remind readers why they trust you, why they follow you, and why they look forward to hearing from you.

Instead of being a task, your newsletter can be a tool. A tool for connection. A tool for growth. A tool for building something that lasts. Make it worth opening every single time.

6 Best Practices of a Successful Newsletter

A great newsletter doesn't happen by accident. It's built on a foundation of consistency, value, and thoughtful planning. When done right, your newsletter becomes more than just an email—it's a trusted resource, a piece of your brand, and a connection point with your audience. Let's break down the key components that will set your newsletter apart.

Best Practice 1. Choose a Day of the Week

Consistency is the bedrock of trust. When your readers know they can count on your email arriving at the same time every week, it creates a sense of reliability. It's not just about showing up; it's about showing up regularly and on time. A sporadic schedule, on the other hand, sends a message that your newsletter isn't a priority—so why should it be a priority for them?

Think about your favorite TV show or podcast. You know exactly when to expect the next episode, and that builds anticipation. Your newsletter should create the same rhythm in your readers' lives. Pick a day, commit to it, and make it non-negotiable.

Best Practice 2. Brand Your Newsletter with a Name

A unique name transforms your newsletter from "just another email" into a branded product. It makes it memorable and gives it an identity. A name like *Monday Messenger* or *The Solopreneur Weekly* feels intentional and polished. It signals to your audience that this is something worth paying attention to.

A great name also sets expectations. It tells readers what your newsletter is about and who it's for. That clarity helps attract the right audience and keeps them engaged. Take time to brainstorm a name that reflects your mission and resonates with your audience—it's a small touch that makes a big difference.

Best Practice 3. Deliver Unmatched Value

Your newsletter should feel like a gift, not an obligation. Every issue should deliver something your audience finds useful or inspiring. This could be actionable advice, behind-the-scenes insights, or even a moment of humor or encouragement. Whatever you choose, the focus must be on the reader, not on you.

When readers feel like you're writing for their benefit, they'll keep opening your emails. On the flip side, newsletters that focus too heavily on selling or self-promotion are a quick way to lose trust.

Your audience isn't there to be sold to; they're there to be served. Make every issue worth their time, and you'll earn their loyalty.

Best Practice 4. Catch Attention with Engaging Subject Lines

The subject line is your first impression. In a crowded inbox, it's the difference between being opened or ignored. A good subject line sparks curiosity and promises value. It doesn't have to be flashy, but it does need to be intentional.

Think of your subject line as a handshake—it sets the tone for everything that follows. Experiment with curiosity-driven phrases, direct benefits, or even playful language. And don't stop there—test what works. Over time, you'll learn what resonates with your audience and fine-tune your approach.

Best Practice 5. Create a Dedicated Landing Page for Your Newsletter

A dedicated opt-in page is more than just a signup form—it's a chance to showcase why your newsletter matters. Highlight the benefits of subscribing, whether it's exclusive insights, practical tips, or behind-the-scenes stories. If you have testimonials or sample content, include them to build trust.

Keep the design simple and focused. The goal is to make it as easy as possible for someone to say yes. Avoid clutter or distractions that might pull attention away from the signup form. When subscribing feels effortless and exciting, more people will join your list.

Best Practice 6. Turn Your Weekly Newsletter into a Lead Magnet

Your weekly newsletter topic is more than just content—it's a powerful lead magnet. Social media becomes the stage where you build anticipation, spark curiosity, and encourage action. By strategically posting before, during, and after your newsletter goes live, you create a cycle that continuously grows your email list.

The day before your newsletter drops, tease the topic. Share a post that hints at the value inside without giving too much away. Use curiosity-driven bullet points or pose a question your audience can't resist answering. For example, "Tomorrow's newsletter reveals the three things holding most entrepreneurs back—are you making these mistakes?" This post piques interest and invites people to subscribe so they don't miss out.

On the day of your newsletter, shift the focus to immediacy. Let your audience know the issue is live and ready for them. A post like "This week's issue is here: [Newsletter Name]! Discover how to [solve a specific problem or gain a benefit]—don't miss it!" creates urgency. Include a clear call-to-action, like a direct link to subscribe and get the issue delivered instantly.

The day after, reach out to those who might have missed it. Frame your post as an opportunity to catch up. For instance, "Yesterday's newsletter uncovered [highlight a key takeaway or unique insight]. If you missed it, subscribe now to get the latest issue and stay ahead next week." This keeps your newsletter top of mind and encourages latecomers to join the list.

These three posts—tease, announce, and follow-up—work together to attract new subscribers every week. By leveraging the weekly topic as a fresh lead magnet, you not only grow your list but also create a sense of momentum and engagement around your newsletter.

Practical Exercise: Build Your Newsletter Strategy

Follow these steps to create a newsletter that builds trust, engages your audience, and grows your email list.

Step 1: Name Your Newsletter

Choose a name that reflects your brand and the value your newsletter provides. A great name turns your newsletter into a brand. It sets clear expectations for your audience.

- Keep it simple and descriptive (e.g., *Monday Messenger*, *The Solopreneur Weekly*).

- Brainstorm 3-5 options and ask for feedback from trusted peers or members of your audience.

Step 2: Commit to a Consistent Schedule

Consistency builds trust. Decide on a specific day and time for sending your newsletter and stick to it. Your audience should know exactly when to expect it.

- Add the schedule to your calendar as a recurring event.

- Set a reminder to prepare the newsletter in advance.

Step 3: Craft Engaging Subject Lines

Your subject line is your hook. It should spark curiosity or highlight a clear benefit to entice readers to open your email.

Write three subject lines for your next newsletter:

- One that creates curiosity: "The Simple Habit That Doubles Your Productivity"

- One that promises a benefit: "How to Save 10 Hours a Week With These 3 Tools"

- One that uses a question: "Are You Making These Common Marketing Mistakes?"

Test your options with a small group of your audience or on social media to see which gets the best response.

Step 4: Create a Social Media Teaser Plan

Use social media to build excitement and attract new subscribers for your newsletter. Each weekly topic becomes a mini-lead magnet when you share it strategically.

- **Day Before Teaser:** "Tomorrow's newsletter reveals [tease the topic]. Subscribe now so you don't miss it!"

- **Day Of Announcement:** "This week's newsletter is live! Learn how to [specific benefit]. Get it instantly—subscribe here."

- **Day After Reminder:** "Missed yesterday's issue? We covered [key takeaway]. Subscribe now to get it and stay ahead next week!"

Write out a draft of these posts and schedule them in advance.

Step 5: Build a Simple Opt-In Page

A dedicated opt-in page makes it easy for readers to subscribe to your newsletter. Highlight what they'll gain by signing up.

- **Headline:** "Weekly Strategies to [Achieve Specific Result]"

- **Benefits List:** "Practical tips, behind-the-scenes insights, and strategies delivered every [day of the week]."

- **Sign-Up Form:** Make it simple with just a name and email field.

Review your page to ensure it's visually clear, mobile-friendly, and quick to load.

This exercise is your roadmap to building a consistent, engaging, and growth-focused newsletter. By completing these steps, you'll have a strategy that not only retains readers but also attracts new ones every week.

Key Takeaways

- A well-executed weekly newsletter builds trust, loyalty, and recurring revenue by delivering consistent value to your audience.

- Treat your newsletter like a branded product with engaging subject lines, actionable content, and a memorable name to stand out.

- Leveraging social media to tease, announce, and follow up on your newsletter topic creates a continuous feedback loop that grows your email list each week.

8

How to Create the Perfect Welcome Email Sequence

It was January of 2021. I attended a talk by Yara Golden, known for her way with words. I wasn't ready for how much her insights would reshape my thinking. She spoke about the power of a good welcome email sequence. It should not just sell. It should warm people up, build trust, and make them feel seen. It wasn't about pushing a product. It was about telling a story, forming a connection, and helping someone feel like they'd found the right place.

Her process struck a nerve. I reached out and asked her team to help me write one of my own. For hours, they grilled me about my life—what brought me to this work, what I'd struggled with, and what I wanted for the people I served. Then, they took everything I told them and turned it into a six-day series of emails for people who bought my book. I wasn't sure what to expect when I plugged it into my funnel, but I'll never forget what happened next.

People emailed me back. Not just once or twice but in droves. They said things like, "I printed these out to reread later," and "This felt like you were speaking directly to me." Those emails weren't just selling a product. They were pulling people in, helping them see themselves in my story, and building something far more valuable than a quick sale—trust.

This experience taught me something that's easy to overlook. Your email list isn't just a list of names. It's people. Each one has dreams, struggles, and questions they need answered. How you show up in their inbox in that first week can make all the difference in whether they stick around or drift away.

Ghosting Your Subscribers: What Most People Get Wrong

Most people treat their email list like a vending machine. Subscribers opt in, and marketers immediately hit them with sales pitches. There's no warm-up, no introduction, no sense of connection. It's like walking up to a stranger at a party and asking them to buy your product before you even say hello. Sure, a few might say yes, but most will walk away, unimpressed and uninterested.

Even worse, many don't bother with a welcome sequence at all. Instead, subscribers are tossed straight into a stream of generic emails that might as well be spam. It's easy to see why this happens. People get excited about making a sale. They forget there's a person on the other end of the email. That person is deciding, consciously or not, whether to trust you.

This approach is not only lazy, but it's also painfully short-sighted. Dean Jackson, an expert in email marketing, conducted a study. It revealed a startling statistic: only 15% of customers buy within 90 days of joining your list. That means a whopping 85% of your potential buyers are hanging out on the sidelines, waiting for the right moment to pull the trigger. When you rush straight into selling, you risk alienating that larger group—85% of the people who could become loyal customers.

Think about the stakes. If you're only focused on immediate sales, you're burning through your list and leaving money on the table. A bad welcome could mean the difference between a sale and an "unsubscribe." Without a proper introduction, you're a door-to-door salesman, not a trusted guide. And trust? That's the currency that really matters.

From Strangers to Friends: A Better Approach

Think about how relationships start. When you meet someone new, you don't dive into a sales pitch about your latest project. You take a moment to introduce yourself, share a little about your life, and maybe tell a story or two. You listen. You find common ground. You build a connection. The best email welcome sequences do exactly the same thing.

A new subscriber isn't just a name in your database—they're a person who's just opened the door to your world. They've raised their hand and said, "I'm interested." But interest isn't the same as trust. Trust takes time. And like any new relationship, the first steps matter the most.

Instead of bombarding them with offers, start by showing them who you are. Share a piece of your story—what brought you to this work, why it matters to you, and how you want to help. Give them a reason to lean in, to feel like they've found someone who gets it, someone they can relate to. This isn't about oversharing or turning your emails into a memoir. It's about giving them a glimpse behind the curtain, enough to spark curiosity and lay the foundation for trust.

When you shift your focus from selling to connecting, everything changes. A good welcome sequence invites subscribers to feel like they belong. It makes them curious to hear more and keeps them opening your emails because they've started to see you as more than just another marketer. They see you as someone who has something meaningful to say. And that's when they start to listen.

The 6-Day Perfect Welcome Sequence Framework

When someone new joins your list, you have a rare and fleeting opportunity to make a first impression. Your welcome sequence isn't just a set of emails; it's your chance to show subscribers that they're in the right place. Over the next six days, you'll guide them through your world, helping them understand who you are, what you do, and why it matters. Think of it as a conversation where trust is built one email at a time.

Each day focuses on a single theme, allowing you to connect, inspire, and leave readers wanting more. This isn't about overwhelming them with information. It's about taking them on a journey—your journey—and inviting them to imagine how it could intersect with their own.

Day 1: Who You Are

Your first email is where it all begins. This is where you let subscribers in, sharing a little bit of your backstory and painting a picture of who you are. Think about the milestones that shaped you—moments that led you to where you are today. Were there pivotal events that made you rethink everything? Were there struggles that defined your perspective? This is the time to share them.

The goal isn't to impress. It's to connect. Readers don't need to know every detail of your life. They need to see the human behind the emails. Maybe you were burned out in a career that didn't fulfill you, or maybe you found yourself facing a challenge that forced you to grow. Whatever your story, let them see the heart behind it. Share the "why" that keeps you going, and give them a glimpse of the passion that drives you to do what you do.

Day 2: What You Do

Now that they know a little about you, it's time to talk about what you do. This isn't about listing your products or services. It's about defining the problem you solve and the transformation you provide. What pain points do you address? What kind of change do you make possible for the people you serve?

Imagine a bridge. On one side is where your audience is now—frustrated, stuck, or overwhelmed. On the other side is where they want to be—empowered, capable, or successful. Your role is the bridge. Explain how you help people cross from one side to the other. Be clear and specific. When subscribers understand the value you bring to the table, they'll start to see why sticking around might just be worth their time.

Day 3: How You Do It

By now, your readers are starting to trust you. They know who you are and what you're about. This is where you explain *how* you deliver results. What's your process? What's your method? You don't need to give away all the details—this isn't the time for a step-by-step tutorial. Instead, focus on the bigger picture.

For example, maybe your approach is rooted in years of trial and error. Or maybe you've distilled complex concepts into a simple, repeatable framework. Whatever sets you apart, make it clear that what you do works—not just for you, but for the people you've helped. Give them confidence in your ability to deliver, and they'll be eager to learn more.

Day 4: How You Learned It

Your expertise didn't appear out of thin air. It's the result of a journey, one that probably included more than a few wrong turns. This is your chance to share that journey. Let them see where you started and how far you've come. Were there moments when you wanted to quit? Times when you doubted yourself? Those struggles are what make your story relatable.

Growth is never easy, and when you share the challenges you've overcome, you're giving your audience something powerful: hope. They'll see that if you can do it, maybe they can too. And that's what makes your expertise so valuable—not just what you've learned, but the path you've taken to get there.

Day 5: Who You Do It For

Your audience wants to see themselves in your story. They want to know that you understand them, that you've walked in their shoes, or that you've helped others who have. This email is where you highlight the people you serve. Share a success story, someone who came to you with a problem and walked away with a solution.

What was their life like before they worked with you? What changed after? Be specific. Results are what build trust. When subscribers see what's possible through your work, they'll start to imagine what's possible for them too. And that's when they'll begin to lean in.

Day 6: How You Can Do It for Them

This is where it all comes together. You've introduced yourself, shared your mission, and shown the transformation you create. Now it's time to turn the focus back on your reader. How can you help them? What's your mission, and how does it align with their goals?

Make this email about them. Paint a picture of what their life could look like if they stick with you. Reinforce the trust you've built over the past five days, and invite them to take the next step. Give them a reason to believe their journey with you is just starting. Whether it's by joining a program, reading your blog, or staying engaged, keep them connected.

Practical Exercise: Crafting Your 6-Day Welcome Sequence

Creating a welcome sequence may seem overwhelming at first, but breaking it into small, manageable steps makes it simpler. Use the prompts below to draft your sequence, one email at a time. Don't worry about perfection—focus on clarity, connection, and authenticity.

Step 1: Who You Are

- Write 3-5 key moments from your life that shaped who you are today.

- Choose one milestone to share in your email. Keep it personal but relevant to your audience.

- End the email with one question that invites readers to reply. Example: *What's one thing that led you to where you are today?*

Step 2: What You Do

- Define the main problem your audience faces. Write this down in one sentence.

- Describe the transformation your work creates. What does life look like after solving this problem?

- Share why this work matters to you. Use emotional language to convey your passion.

Step 3: How You Do It

- List the steps or principles behind your process. Aim for 3-5 steps.

- Write one paragraph summarizing how your method works.

- Think about what makes your approach unique. Add a sentence that highlights this distinction.

Step 4: How You Learned It

- Reflect on the struggles you overcame to gain your expertise. Write down one key story.

- Include a turning point where everything began to click for you.

- End with a sentence that explains why this journey matters to your readers.

Step 5: Who You Do It For

- Write a brief description of your ideal audience.

- Recall one person you've helped and outline their story. Start with their challenge, highlight the solution, and finish with the result.

- End with a sentence inviting readers to see themselves in that story.

Step 6: How You Can Do It for Them

- Write a sentence about your mission or "why."

- List one or two specific ways you can help your audience.

- End with a call to action. Example: *If this resonates with you, here's how I can help you get started.*

Step 7: Review Your Draft

After writing each email, step back and read it aloud. Does it feel personal? Does it reflect your voice? Make sure each email builds trust and curiosity, leaving readers eager for what's next.

Key Takeaways

- A thoughtful welcome sequence helps build trust and connection with new subscribers, setting the foundation for long-term relationships.

- Sharing your story and demonstrating empathy can make subscribers feel seen, understood, and valued, which keeps them engaged.

- Nurturing relationships before making a sales pitch increases the likelihood of future conversions and strengthens loyalty.

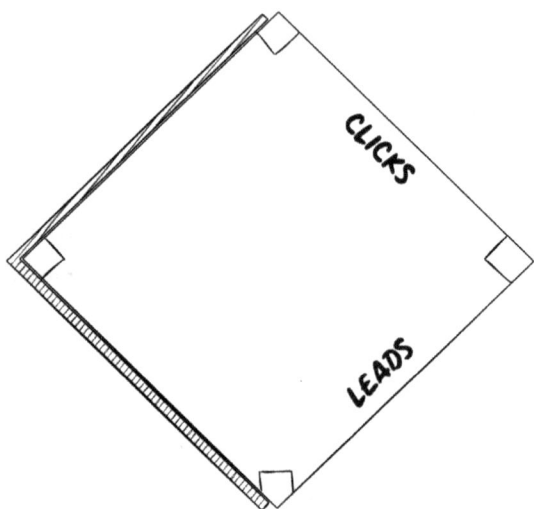

Second Base:
Engaging Clicks

9

Second Base: Engaging Clicks

S wayChic was just another clothing retailer struggling to break through the noise. Their emails were like billboards on a crowded highway—ignored and uninspired. Then they tried something new. They began segmenting their subscribers based on what they cared about most. Shoppers interested in dresses got emails about the newest arrivals. Bargain hunters received updates about exclusive sales. The results? Their average open rates jumped by 40%. Click-through rates doubled. Revenue per campaign tripled.[4]

It wasn't magic. It was relevance. SwayChic proved that when people feel understood, they engage.

Think about your email list. It's not one big audience—it's a collection of individuals. Each subscriber has unique interests, problems, and desires. But most email marketers send the same promotions to everyone, hoping something sticks. That's where things go wrong.

This chapter introduces a game-changing concept: Click Magnets. Unlike lead magnets, these resources don't ask for opt-ins. They're crafted for subscribers who are already on your list. When someone clicks on a link to access a checklist, worksheet, or video, they raise their hand and say, "This interests me." That click becomes a signal. It's your opportunity to segment, personalize, and automate in a way that feels effortless and natural.

The secret is in the strategy. Click Magnets allow you to move beyond generic marketing and start conversations that resonate. They're the bridge between trust and action, engagement and sales. This isn't just about improving metrics—it's about transforming relationships.

Why One-Size-Fits-All Emails Don't Work

Many email marketers treat their lists as a single group, sending the same promotions to everyone without distinction. It's an easy approach but one that misses the mark.

Let's say you walk into a car dealership, and the salesperson is trying to sell a truck to everyone who walks through the door. A commuter wants a fuel-efficient sedan. A family seeks a spacious SUV. An enthusiast looks for a sports car. Each one hears the same pitch. It's a recipe for frustration and lost opportunities.

When every subscriber gets the same message, it's like offering a random solution to a problem they may not have. Subscribers feel disconnected.

Relevance is everything. Without it, your emails feel like noise. Subscribers start to ignore them, assuming there's nothing valuable for them inside. Trust erodes when people feel like you don't understand their needs.

This lack of connection doesn't just hurt relationships—it impacts your results. Open rates slide. Click-throughs decline. And sales stall before they even begin.

Shifting the Focus

The key to engaging your email list isn't selling to everyone—it's listening first. Instead of blasting out promotions to the whole list, aim to create opportunities for subscribers to show you what they're interested in.

This is where Click Magnets come in. They're not about pushing a product. They're about providing something valuable—like a checklist, guide, or video—and using that value to spark a response. When a subscriber clicks, they're raising their hand and saying, "This matters to me."

That simple action does more than grab attention. It gives you insight. Each click is a signal you can use to segment your list, personalize your messages, and guide the right people into an automated sales sequence. It's subtle, effective, and far more engaging than treating everyone the same.

The Second Base Email Strategy: Turning Clicks Into Conversions

Click Magnets work because they're not about selling—they're about starting a conversation. To make them effective, you need a system that turns clicks into deeper connections. This process isn't complicated, but each piece is essential. Here's how to create a streamlined approach that ensures every click counts.

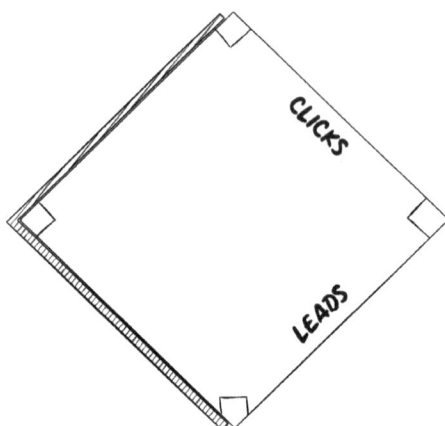

Create an Automated Sales Sequence

Automation is the backbone of this strategy. When a subscriber clicks on your Click Magnet, they should automatically enter a pre-written sales sequence. This sequence, typically 3-5 days long, does the heavy lifting for you.

An evergreen sales sequence is timeless. It's designed to work repeatedly, no matter when a subscriber engages. For example, if your Click Magnet is a checklist for writing a book, your sequence might introduce your writing course over a series of emails. Each email builds on the last. It highlights benefits, shares success stories, and addresses common objections.

Why start here? Because every click is a signal of interest. Automating your follow-up ensures a quick, consistent response. It turns warm leads into paying customers without constant manual effort.

Create Your Click Magnet

Your Click Magnet is the spark that ignites engagement. It's not about being flashy—it's about being valuable. Think about what your ideal customer would find helpful. Is it a cheat sheet for achieving a specific goal? A starter guide to simplify a process? A training video that answers a pressing question?

Whatever you choose, it should connect directly to what you're offering in your sales sequence. For example, if you're promoting a book-writing course, a checklist for outlining a bestseller could be the perfect Click Magnet. Keep it simple, focused, and action-oriented. Subscribers should feel like they're getting a shortcut to something they care about.

Write a Broadcast Email

The way you introduce your Click Magnet to your list matters. A broadcast email is your chance to frame the resource as something genuinely helpful, not a gimmick.

Write 1-3 emails that tell a story, share a lesson, or solve a problem. For example, if your Click Magnet is a social media checklist, start your email with a relatable story about being overwhelmed by content creation. Then, transition into how your checklist simplifies the process and makes it manageable.

The goal isn't to sell. It's to spark curiosity and create an "aha" moment for your subscribers. By focusing on value, you're building trust while naturally encouraging clicks.

Set Up Your Automation

Automation ensures every click leads to action. When a subscriber engages with your Click Magnet, your email marketing software should tag them and add them to your sales sequence.

Tags act like digital breadcrumbs. If someone clicks on your check-list link, you might tag them as "Interested: Writing Checklist." From there, you set up a rule: when this tag is added, the subscriber is automatically placed into the writing course sales sequence.

Automation isn't just efficient—it's smart. It allows you to tailor your messages without lifting a finger. Subscribers get content tailored to their interests, not a generic email blast.

Create a Click Magnet Database

As you create more Click Magnets, staying organized becomes crit-ical. A simple spreadsheet can save you time and effort in the long run.

In your database, track key details like the Click Magnet's name, topic, associated tags, and the sales sequence it feeds into.

Reusing Click Magnets is another reason to stay organized. New subscribers join your list all the time, and older subscribers may not have seen your previous emails. By keeping a clear record, you can reintroduce valuable resources and maximize their reach.

Practical Exercise: Drafting Your Click Magnet Plan

This exercise will help you outline a complete Click Magnet strategy, from start to finish, without getting bogged down in the details. By the end, you'll have a draft plan ready to implement. Focus on brainstorming ideas and angles rather than perfecting every detail.

Step 1: Define Your Sales Sequence

- Identify the product or service you want to promote.

- Example: If you're promoting a book-writing course, write that at the top of your plan.

- Outline a 3-5 day email sequence that aligns with your offer.

  - Email 1: Introduce the problem your product solves.

  - Email 2: Share a success story or a common mistake your audience can avoid.

  - Email 3: Present your product or service as the solution.

  - Email 4: Highlight benefits or address common objections.

  - Email 5: Create urgency with a limited-time bonus or reminder.

Step 2: Design Your Click Magnet

- Choose a resource that aligns with your product and delivers quick value.

  - Examples: A checklist, cheat sheet, starter guide, or short training video.

- Write down the title or idea for your Click Magnet.

  - Example: "10 Steps to Outline Your Bestseller in a Day" (for a writing course).

- List 2-3 reasons why this resource will grab your audience's attention.

  - Example: It's actionable, solves a specific pain point, and connects directly to the product.

Step 3: Draft Your Broadcast Emails

- Brainstorm the main angle for each email.

  ○ Email 1: Share a relatable story about struggling with the problem your Click Magnet solves.

  ○ Email 2: Highlight the benefits of the Click Magnet and how it simplifies the reader's life.

  ○ Email 3: Provide social proof or a compelling reason why they shouldn't miss this resource.

- Write the first sentence for each email to set the tone.

  ○ Example: "Ever feel like you're spinning your wheels trying to get started on your book?"

Next Steps

- Review your plan and identify any gaps or areas that need more thought.

- Set a deadline for completing the emails, creating the Click Magnet, and setting up automation.

- Start small. Test this strategy with one Click Magnet and adjust based on the results.

By drafting the big ideas first, you'll have a clear roadmap for creating your Click Magnet strategy without feeling overwhelmed.

Key Takeaways

- Segmenting your email list by interest leads to better engagement and higher sales.

- Click Magnets help identify subscribers' interests without making hard sales pitches.

- Automation and tagging allow for efficient, scalable personalization in email marketing.

10

Email Subject Lines (Get Your Emails Opened)

"**H**ey." One word. That was the subject line that helped Barack Obama's 2012 re-election campaign raise $690 million through email donations. It wasn't flashy or formal. It didn't scream, "Urgent!" or "Click now!" It simply said, "Hey."

Why did it work? It felt personal, like a text from a friend. It caught people off guard in a sea of formal, bland emails. It piqued curiosity. Who wouldn't want to know what a message titled "Hey" was about?

Obama's campaign team tested countless subject lines, from long and detailed to short and mysterious. Time and again, the simpler, more casual lines won. This wasn't luck. It was intentional. They understood that the subject line is the first impression, the hook that gets an email opened. Without it, the best content in the world might as well be invisible.[5]

Subject lines matter because they unlock the door to your email. They're your one shot at grabbing attention in a crowded, chaotic inbox. If your email isn't opened, your message goes unheard. No engagement. No clicks. No sales.

This chapter is all about that crucial first impression. It's about knowing the power of email subject lines. It's about learning to create ones that stand out, get noticed, and, most importantly, get opened. Because if your emails don't get opened, they can't do their job. And that's a problem you can't afford to ignore.

The Graveyard of Generic Subject Lines

Most people treat email subject lines like afterthoughts. They'll slap on something lifeless like "Newsletter Issue #25" or "Weekly Update." Sure, it's clear, but it's also painfully dull. Others take the opposite route, cramming their subject lines with exclamation points, ALL CAPS, or desperate phrases like "Act NOW!!!"

Neither approach works.

Boring subject lines fade into the sea of sameness, while over-the-top ones come off as insincere. Both fail to do the one thing a subject line must do: make someone curious enough to click. Without that spark, even the most brilliant email content will go unread.

Why Your Subject Line Never Gets Invited to the Party

Think of your inbox like a VIP event—only the most intriguing guests make it past the velvet rope. A generic subject line like "Weekly Update" doesn't exactly scream "exclusive." It's predictable. Easy to skip. Readers don't open emails to feel bored—they open them because they're curious or compelled.

Then there's the other extreme: spammy subject lines. Those loud, flashy phrases that try way too hard to grab attention. All caps, endless punctuation, or misleading promises don't just turn people off—they erode trust. Worse, they can land your email in the spam folder, where no one ever goes to look.

The truth is, you've got one shot to grab attention in a noisy inbox. A subject line isn't just a label—it's a first impression. And if it doesn't make someone stop and click, your email might as well be invisible.

The Secret to Standout Subject Lines

A great subject line doesn't happen by accident. It's crafted with intention, built to speak directly to your audience's emotions and interests. Think about it—what makes you open an email? Maybe it promises something valuable. Maybe it makes you curious. Or maybe it feels like it was written just for you.

Your audience isn't any different. They're busy, distracted, and constantly making snap judgments about what's worth their time. To grab their attention, your subject line needs to feel personal, relevant, and impossible to ignore. It means knowing what your audience cares about. You must tap into their emotions. This includes curiosity, urgency, excitement, and a bit of FOMO.

Crack the C.U.B.E.: Four Styles of Subject Lines That Get Clicked

Your subject line isn't just a headline—it's an invitation. A good subject line can grab attention. It can tease a secret, promise value, or tug at the heartstrings. To master this, you need a framework that keeps you intentional and creative. Enter the C.U.B.E. method: Curiosity, Urgency, Benefit, and Emotional. Each style works differently, but all are proven to get results.

Let's explore how each one works and why they matter. Along the way, you'll find practical insights and examples to guide your next email campaign.

Curiosity-Driven Subject Lines

Curiosity is a powerful tool. It taps into an instinctive need to know the answer, like a door slightly ajar, tempting you to peek inside. Subject lines that spark curiosity create an irresistible pull, urging readers to open your email to see what's hidden.

For example, consider: *"You won't believe what happened yesterday..."* It's vague but intriguing. It leaves questions unanswered. What happened? Why should I care? The beauty of curiosity-driven subject lines is that they're not about giving information—they're about withholding it. The less you reveal, the stronger the urge to click.

But beware: curiosity without relevance can backfire. If your subject line feels like a bait-and-switch, readers will lose trust. Make sure the content of your email delivers on the intrigue you've created. When done right, curiosity builds excitement and fosters engagement.

Urgency-Driven Subject Lines

People hate missing out. Urgency-driven subject lines capitalize on this by creating a sense of scarcity or time sensitivity. They push readers to act now rather than later—or worse, never. Phrases like *"TIME SENSITIVE: Doors Close Tonight!"* trigger a feeling of "if I don't open this now, I might regret it."

These subject lines work best when there's a real deadline or a limited opportunity. In the final phase of an evergreen sales campaign, urgency can boost last-minute conversions. But timing matters. Overusing urgency can dilute its impact, making it feel less credible over time.

Think of urgency like salt in a recipe—just enough enhances the flavor, but too much ruins the dish. Reserve this style for moments when you truly need your audience to act fast. When used sparingly and strategically, urgency-driven subject lines can make all the difference in closing a sale.

Benefit-Driven Subject Lines

Sometimes, the simplest approach is the most effective. Benefit-driven subject lines tell readers exactly what they'll gain by opening your email. They answer the question: "What's in it for me?"

Take *"FREE: Step-by-Step Blueprint Inside"* as an example. It's clear, direct, and promises value. There's no guesswork involved. Readers know what they're getting, and if the offer aligns with their needs, they're far more likely to click.

The key to benefit-driven subject lines is specificity. Vague promises like "Learn something amazing!" won't cut it. Instead, focus on tangible results or concrete takeaways. If your audience knows they're getting something actionable, they'll reward you with their attention. Clarity wins here, every time.

Emotional-Driven Subject Lines

Emotions drive decisions. Subject lines that tap into feelings—whether it's curiosity, guilt, humor, or nostalgia—create deep connections. *"Did I do something wrong?"* is a perfect example. It plays on guilt or concern, compelling readers to click and find out more.

Emotionally-driven subject lines don't have to be negative. They can evoke joy, excitement, or even a sense of belonging. Phrases like

"You're not alone in this..." create a personal connection, making the email feel more like a conversation than a sales pitch.

The trick is to align your emotional appeal with your audience's mindset. If they're stressed, offer comfort. If they're ambitious, spark excitement. Emotions are powerful levers—pull the right one, and you'll see a noticeable lift in engagement.

Testing and Iteration: Refining the Formula

Even with the best subject lines, there's no one-size-fits-all. That's why testing is essential. A/B testing lets you see what resonates with your audience, so you can refine your approach.

Using tools like Kajabi's A/B testing feature, you can split your list and send two subject line variations to a small segment. For example, 25% of your audience gets *"Exclusive Offer Ends Tonight,"* while another 25% sees *"Time-Sensitive: 24 Hours Left."* Four hours later, the subject line with the most clicks is sent to the remaining 50%.

Clicks, not just opens, should guide your decisions. Why? Because clicks reflect deeper engagement—they show readers are not only interested but ready to act. These tests provide a wealth of insights. They help you understand your audience and craft high-performing subject lines.

Testing isn't just about finding what works—it's about continuously learning and improving. With each iteration, you get closer to unlocking the perfect subject line.

Practical Exercise: Create Your First A/B Test

Writing a winning subject line takes intentional effort and creativity. This exercise will guide you. It will help you to craft, test, and refine subject lines. These should resonate with your audience and boost email engagement.

Start by writing your email. It's easier to craft a compelling subject line when you know the content and purpose of your message. Don't rush this step. A clear understanding of what your email offers will inspire better subject lines.

Step 1: Brainstorm Using the C.U.B.E. Method

After completing your email, brainstorm at least four subject line variations. Use the C.U.B.E. framework to ensure variety:

- **Curiosity**: Think of a line that teases the email content without giving too much away. Example: *"What I learned after 3 failed launches..."*

- **Urgency**: Create a subject line that emphasizes time sensitivity. Example: *"Last chance to grab this offer—ends tonight!"*

- **Benefit**: Highlight the value the email provides. Example: *"Free toolkit: Write better emails in 10 minutes"*

- **Emotional**: Tap into feelings to create a personal connection. Example: *"Are you making this email mistake?"*

Writing multiple options helps you explore different angles and increases the chance of finding a winner. I always brainstorm at least ten email subject lines before I choose the two I like best. Then I move onto split testing.

Step 2: Test Your Subject Lines with A/B Testing

Use your email platform's A/B testing feature to test two of your brainstormed subject lines. For example, send a curiosity-driven subject line and a benefit-driven one. Do this to two smaller segments of your audience (e.g., 25% each).

Choose a clear timeframe for your test—four hours works well for most campaigns. Focus on measuring **clicks** rather than just opens. Clicks indicate deeper engagement and a stronger connection with your audience.

Step 3: Analyze and Learn from the Results

Once the test concludes, review the results to see which subject line performed better. Pay attention to patterns. Did curiosity generate more clicks? Did urgency fall flat? The insights you gather will help you refine future subject lines.

Send the winning subject line to the rest of your list, confident that it will perform well. Over time, keep a record of your top-performing subject lines to build a library of proven approaches.

Key Takeaways

- Subject lines are your email's first impression—make them count.

- Test and refine your subject lines to discover what resonates with your audience.

- Use curiosity, emotion, and clear benefits to increase your open rates.

11

The Daily Story Email Explained

T he morning light streamed through the window as I reached for my phone. There it was—a notification that stopped me cold. Someone had purchased my product overnight. The excitement was electric. I sat up, heart pounding, as I realized the dream was real. While I slept, my work had resonated with someone, enough for them to take action and invest in what I offered. That moment was unforgettable.

Why was it so powerful? It wasn't just about the sale. It was the connection. My message had reached someone, solved a problem for them, and made them feel seen. It felt deeply personal, even though I didn't know the buyer.

Now, imagine the opposite. An email crammed with cold, impersonal details. No story, no emotion—just facts, pitches, or endless tips. It's forgettable, isn't it? When emails lack a personal touch, they fall flat. Readers don't engage, and they definitely don't take action.

This chapter dives into why so many emails fail to inspire. It's not because you didn't try hard enough. It's because connection was missing. And when there's no connection, your audience tunes out, leaving your emails unread or deleted. Let's explore what's going wrong—and how to fix it.

Why Most Emails Fail to Stick

Long emails full of endless details. That's what most people send. They think cramming value into every corner of their email will impress readers. But instead, it overwhelms them. Like trying to drink from a firehose, readers get blasted with too much information. They skim. They close the email. They move on.

Some lean hard into promotions. Every email screams, "Buy this now!" No context, no connection—just a hard sell. Readers sense it immediately. It feels cold, impersonal, and desperate. It's like being cornered by a pushy salesperson when all you wanted was to browse.

Then there's the third group. They forget stories altogether. No drama, no emotion, no humanity. Just bland updates or facts. Without a story, emails become white noise. They're easy to delete, easy to forget, and never stand out.

The common thread? None of these approaches create a connection. None build trust. And without trust, your audience won't take action.

Why Your Emails Aren't Inspiring Action

When emails overflow with information, it's exhausting. Readers don't know where to focus. Should they act on the first tip? The second? The tenth? Decision fatigue sets in, and instead of engaging, they opt out. It's like standing in front of a buffet so overwhelming that you lose your appetite.

Sales pitches that never let up feel like a battering ram. Readers start to brace themselves every time they see your name in their inbox. Trust erodes little by little. Instead of being excited to hear from you, they dread it. No one wants to feel like a walking dollar sign.

Without a story to guide them, your emails lack life. Facts and updates on their own are hollow. They don't stir emotion or curiosity. Without connection, there's no reason for readers to stick around. A story is the glue that holds their attention, and without it, your message falls flat.

These missteps push people away. They drain energy, damage relationships, and leave readers unengaged. For emails to work, they need to do the opposite: energize, connect, and inspire.

How to Make Your Emails Irresistible

Start by becoming an attractive character. People don't connect with brands; they connect with people. Share stories from your life—those small, relatable moments that reveal your personality. A morning walk with your dog, a lesson learned from a setback, or an aha moment sparked by a simple observation. These stories make you real, approachable, and memorable.

Stories aren't just for entertainment—they're bridges. A good story grabs attention and holds it. It lets readers see themselves in your experiences. But the key is to connect the story to your offer. Whether it's a free checklist or a workshop invite, the story lays the groundwork. It transforms your pitch into a natural next step, not a jarring sales interruption.

Emotions are the gateway. A compelling story stirs curiosity, joy, or even nostalgia. Once readers are emotionally invested, they're open to the next step. That's when logic steps in. Your offer makes sense because it's tied to a lesson they just experienced. This shift feels seamless and leaves readers feeling understood and inspired—not sold to.

By focusing on connection first and action second, you'll turn your emails into something readers look forward to opening.

6 Key Principles of Story-Based Emails

Every time I sit down to write a story-based email I follow a simple 6-step script. Adding these elements to your emails will make your subscribers enjoy reading them. To make this memorable, I use an acronym using the word S.T.O.R.Y.

S - Start with Action

Drop readers right into the action. Start with the moment that sparks curiosity and pulls them in. Immediately place them into the high point of drama in the story. Skip the buildup and give them the good stuff upfront. Think of it like a Jason Bourne movie—opening with a high-speed car chase before explaining why it's happening. Readers want to be hooked immediately, not warmed up slowly.

T - Tie in the Scene

Once you've got their attention, set the scene. Introduce the characters, the setting, and the challenge you faced. Keep it tight. Just a few sentences are enough to give them the full picture. The goal is to make it relatable and real.

O - Offer the Lesson

Every great story teaches something. Once the scene is set, deliver the lesson. Make it crystal clear and directly tied to the story you just told. **Bold it for emphasis so it jumps off the screen.** When your readers walk away with a valuable insight, they're more likely to stay engaged.

R – Relate to the Offer

This is where you connect the dots. Use an "if-then" statement to make the transition smooth and logical. For example, "If this lesson resonates with you, check out [offer]." It doesn't feel forced because it's a natural extension of the story.

Y – Your Reader's Next Step

Stories warm readers up and create trust. By the time you introduce an offer, it feels like a natural next step. They're already invested in the value you're sharing, so the offer isn't a push—it's an opportunity.

Not every story needs a direct sales pitch. Sometimes, the goal is just to get readers clicking. Maybe it's a free checklist or a simple resource. The click itself tells you they're interested. And that's valuable information for targeting follow-ups later.

Stories don't just tell—they sell, but in a way that feels personal and genuine. When done right, your emails become more than just messages—they become moments your readers won't forget.

Practical Exercise: Crafting Your Story Email

1. Think of a Relatable Story

- Recall a moment from your life that taught you a lesson. It could be something small, like a realization during a morning routine, or something bigger, like overcoming a challenge. Focus on moments your audience can see themselves in.

2. **Start at the High Point of Drama**

   ○ Write your opening sentence as if you're dropping your reader into the middle of the action. Skip the backstory for now. Hook their curiosity.

   ○ Example: "My heart sank as the professor's words echoed in my head: 'You're not cut out to be a writer.'"

3. **Fill in the Context**

   ○ In 3-5 sentences, explain the setting, who was involved, and why it mattered. Keep it brief but vivid enough for readers to picture the scene.

   ○ Example: "I was sitting in a college classroom, surrounded by aspiring writers. The professor's critique hit harder than I expected, and for weeks, I couldn't shake the feeling that I'd failed."

4. **Highlight the Lesson**

   ○ Clearly state the insight or takeaway from the story. Make it bold so it stands out.

   ○ Example: **Sometimes the most painful feedback becomes the foundation for your greatest growth.**

5. **Transition to an Offer**

   ○ Write an "if-then" statement that ties the lesson to your offer.

   ○ Example: "If you've ever doubted yourself but still feel called to share your story, download my free guide to starting your writing journey."

6. Test Your Email

- Share your draft with a friend, colleague, or mentor. Ask if the story drew them in and if the offer felt natural.

- Revise based on their feedback to make it more engaging and clear.

7. Send and Measure Results

- Pick a segment of your email list and send your story email. Track open rates, clicks, and replies to see how it resonates. Use the data to refine future emails.

This exercise helps you connect with your audience. It delivers value and guides them to take the next step. Do this while being authentic and relatable.

Key Takeaways

- Stories create connection and trust, making your emails engaging and memorable.

- A well-crafted story naturally leads readers to your offer without feeling salesy.

- Emotional engagement through storytelling increases the likelihood of action and deeper audience loyalty.

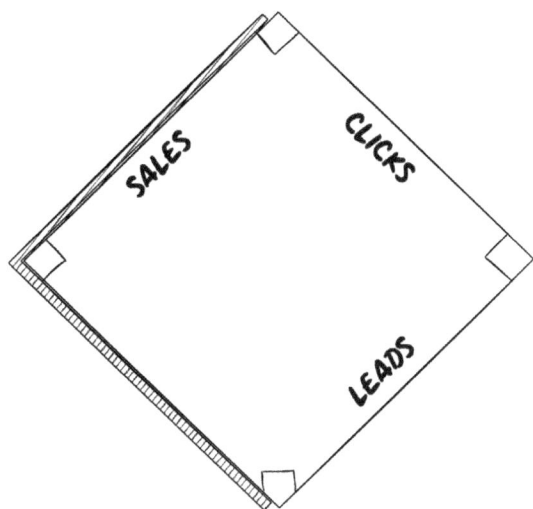

Third Base:
Gaining Sales

12

Third Base: Turning Clicks into Sales

echSoup Polska faced a challenge many businesses know all too well. They needed to help non-profits access affordable technology, but their efforts weren't landing. Their emails went out to everyone on their list with the same message, and the results were lackluster. Then everything changed.

In just one year, they saw a 1200% jump in order value. The key wasn't louder marketing or bigger discounts. It was smarter email sequences. They shifted their focus to delivering the right content to the right people at the right time. They stopped trying to sell to everyone and started becoming a trusted guide for those who needed their help the most.

Their strategy? Understanding subscribers' needs like a friend who really listens. Balancing automation with a human touch. Putting relationships first, sales second.[6]

This chapter is about doing the same thing for your email list. It's about turning clicks into sales—not by pushing harder, but by serving smarter. Segment your list by interest. Then, lead interested subscribers through an automated sales sequence. Something magical happens. Your audience feels understood. Your sales start to grow. And your offers don't fall on deaf ears.

Let's unpack how to make this happen.

The Click-Blind Approach

Most email marketers fall into the same trap: treating their list like a single crowd instead of a group of individuals. Imagine shouting a single message into a packed room, hoping everyone hears it and acts on it. That's what happens when you send the same email to everyone on your list.

The Problem with Copy-Paste Messaging

When every subscriber gets the same email, the message becomes noise. Some people might not care about your latest offer. Others might already know about it. The rest might be interested—but not right now.

It's like handing out sunscreen to people indoors. Sure, it's useful for someone, someday—but right now, it's just clutter.

Overloading with Off-Target Offers

Now add irrelevant offers to the mix. Promotions for products your audience doesn't want or need. Messages with no connection to their current interests. Instead of building trust, these emails chip away at it.

Think about your inbox. How often do you delete emails without opening them? How fast do you unsubscribe when things stop feeling relevant? Your audience does the same thing.

What Happens When You Miss the Mark

- **Email Fatigue**: Even your most loyal subscribers start ignoring your emails when they feel generic.

- **Engagement Plummets**: Open rates sink. Clicks dry up. Your best content gets overlooked.

- **Unsubscribes Climb**: People leave your list not because they don't like you—but because they've stopped seeing the value in sticking around.

Why Generic Emails Backfire

Irrelevance is a deal-breaker. When people open an email, they're looking for one thing: value. If they don't find it, they'll move on—and fast. Generic emails tell your audience, "I don't really know you."

Trust Erodes with Every Missed Connection

Think of your emails as a conversation. A generic message feels like someone talking at you, not to you. It's impersonal. It doesn't connect. Over time, your subscribers start tuning out, and your ability to influence them disappears.

Lost Opportunity to Build Loyalty

When your emails feel off the mark, subscribers aren't just disengaged—they're disappointed. And disappointed people rarely buy.

When your emails try to speak to everyone, they end up speaking to no one. The cost? Lost trust, lost attention, and ultimately, lost sales.

The Secret to Selling Without Selling

The magic happens when your emails stop feeling like marketing and start feeling like a conversation. Instead of treating your list as a single, faceless group, you can create smaller, interest-based segments. Each segment becomes a tailored audience, ready to hear the messages that matter to them.

When you focus on what your subscribers actually care about, everything changes. You're no longer guessing what they need—you know. This lets you send automated emails that guide interested subscribers on a personalized journey.

It's not about selling harder. It's about serving smarter. When you meet your audience where they are, the results speak for themselves.

Third Base: The Evergreen Automated Email Sales Sequence

If you've ever wondered why your emails aren't converting, it's not because your audience isn't interested—it's because you're not meeting them where they are. The key isn't in louder sales pitches or more frequent emails. It's in creating a journey that feels seamless, relevant, and personal. By combining story-driven engagement, smart segmentation, and purposeful automation, you can turn curiosity into commitment.

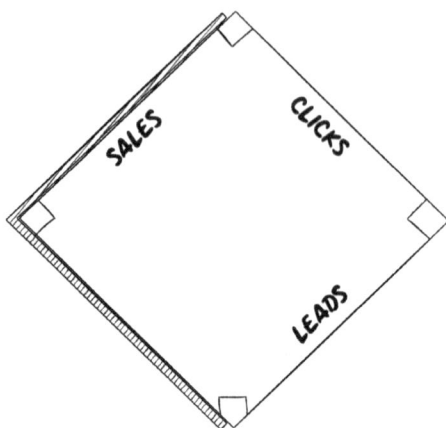

Let's explore the strategies that make this possible.

Step 1. Send Story-Based Emails with Click Magnets

People love stories. They're hardwired to connect with a good narrative. But stories in email marketing aren't just about entertaining—they're about sparking curiosity. When you use a story to frame a problem and offer a free resource as the solution, you're creating what's known as a click magnet.

For example, imagine you're writing to an audience interested in self-publishing. Start with a story about an author who struggled to finish their book because they didn't have a clear plan. Then, introduce a free "Book Writing Checklist" as the exact tool that helped them overcome the challenge. The story pulls the reader in, while the checklist makes them feel like the hero of their own journey.

Click magnets don't just attract clicks—they qualify your audience. Only the subscribers genuinely interested in the topic will take the next step, giving you a focused group to nurture.

Step 2. Add Segmentation Tags

When someone clicks on your click magnet, it's like raising their hand to say, "I'm interested." But that's only useful if you know how to capture and act on that interest. This is where segmentation tags come in.

Segmentation tags are like labels that help you track your subscribers' behaviors. For instance, clicking your "Book Writing Checklist" tags them as interested in book writing. This tag becomes the key to delivering emails that align with their specific needs.

Without tags, your list becomes a jumbled mess of mixed interests. Tags let you speak directly to the people who care about what you're offering. It's like sorting books into genres in a library—everyone can find what they're looking for without getting overwhelmed.

Step 3. Move to Automated Sales Sequences

Once someone shows interest, don't leave them hanging. This is the moment to guide them into an automated sales sequence—a series of emails that builds trust and gently moves them toward a purchase.

Think of it as a conversation that unfolds over time. Start by addressing their pain points, then offer proof that your solution works. Finally, present your product as the logical next step. A sequence of 3-7 emails can tell a story and provide social proof. It won't overwhelm the reader.

Automation takes the pressure off. You don't have to manually follow up with every lead. Instead, your system works behind the scenes, delivering the right message at the right time.

Step 4. Incorporate Evergreen Deadlines

Urgency is a powerful motivator, but it has to feel authentic. Evergreen deadlines let you create real-time urgency for every subscriber based on when they enter your sales sequence. Tools like Deadline Funnel make this easy by starting a personalized timer the moment someone joins.

For example, if your sales sequence is five days long, the timer might count down to an exclusive offer that expires at the end. Once the deadline passes, access to the offer is automatically removed. This creates a sense of "now or never" that encourages action without feeling gimmicky.

Evergreen deadlines turn interest into decisions. By combining urgency with relevance, you give your audience a reason to act today—not someday.

These strategies aren't just about selling—they're about serving your audience in a way that feels personal and purposeful. When done well, your emails stop feeling like marketing and start feeling like a solution your audience has been waiting for.

Practical Exercise: Building Your First Segmented Sales Sequence

It's time to put these strategies into action. Follow these steps to start turning clicks into sales by creating your first segmented email sequence.

1. Audit Your Current List

- Open your email platform and review your list.

- Look for trends in subscriber behavior—what links are they clicking? What free resources or offers have they downloaded?

- Write down 2-3 interests or behaviors that stand out as common among your subscribers.

2. Create a Click Magnet

- Think about a simple, valuable resource that aligns with one of these interests.

- Examples: A checklist, a short guide, or a cheat sheet.

- Design the resource in an easy-to-share format, like a PDF.

3. Set Up Segmentation Tags

- In your email platform, create a tag for subscribers who engage with your click magnet.

- Example: If your click magnet is a "Book Writing Checklist," the tag could be: Interested: Book Writing.

- Link this tag to an automation trigger in your email workflow.

4. Write a Simple Sales Sequence

- Draft 3-7 emails that will go to anyone tagged through your click magnet.

- Start by introducing the problem your audience faces, then share stories or proof, and end with an invitation to purchase.

○ Keep your emails conversational, concise, and focused on the subscriber's needs.

5. Add an Evergreen Deadline

○ Choose a tool like Deadline Funnel or a similar platform to set up personalized timers.

○ Tie the timer to your sales sequence so subscribers see the urgency without feeling pressured.

○ Set clear expectations for what happens after the deadline.

Your goal isn't perfection; it's progress. Start with one segment, one click magnet, and one sequence. As you refine this process, you'll start seeing how segmentation and automation transform your email marketing. Every step brings you closer to creating emails that sell without selling.

Key Takeaways

• Segmentation makes your emails more relevant and engaging, leading to higher conversions.

• Automated sales sequences save time while building trust and guiding subscribers toward a purchase.

• Using urgency thoughtfully with evergreen deadlines encourages action without feeling pushy.

13

The Psychology of Sales Emails

In the 1950s, Coca-Cola found itself in a unique situation. Soda sales typically dipped after the holiday season, and they needed a way to keep the momentum going. So, they launched a clever New Year campaign. The idea was simple: create a limited-time promotion to encourage people to stock up on Coke for their New Year's celebrations. The result? A surge in sales, far beyond what anyone expected. By limiting the time people had to take advantage of the offer, Coca-Cola tapped into a powerful human impulse—the fear of missing out.

Scarcity isn't just a buzzword; it's baked into how we make decisions. When something feels exclusive or fleeting, we want it even more. Coca-Cola proved that urgency, paired with a sense of limited availability, can drive action in ways pure logic never will. This story is just one example of how psychology shapes the way people respond to offers.[7]

The same principles that worked for Coca-Cola decades ago can work for your email list today. Emails that convert don't just list facts or features. They tap into how people think, feel, and decide. They use timeless persuasion principles to inspire action. These are scarcity, urgency, social proof, and reciprocity.

But there's more to it than just sprinkling in a few persuasive phrases. Not every subscriber is wired the same way. Some act on impulse, others want all the facts. Some are motivated by what others think, while others need a looming deadline to finally take the leap. If you want to see real results, you need to know how to reach each type of buyer on your list.

This chapter will show you how to do just that.

Why Most Sales Emails Miss the Mark

The biggest mistake people make with sales emails is treating them like a checklist of product features. Their emails read like instruction manuals. They are packed with specs, features, and dry details. They assume readers care about every bell and whistle. But here's the truth: they don't. Readers aren't scrolling through your email hoping to learn about all the ways your product is better. They're scanning to see how it solves *their* problem.

What's missing in these emails is the emotional hook. People don't buy features; they buy outcomes. They buy what the product will make them feel—relief, confidence, excitement, belonging. When you only focus on the rational side of the equation, like "Our app has advanced reporting features," you leave out the part that actually drives action. Imagine instead saying, "Feel in control of your business with reports that help you spot opportunities before anyone else." Same feature, completely different emotional appeal.

The other common problem? A complete lack of psychological triggers. Humans are wired to respond to scarcity, urgency, and social proof. When these are absent, your email is easy to ignore. A rational appeal like, "Our product saves you time," is fine. But, pair it with urgency: "Act now to save an extra hour every day starting today." This gives people a reason to act now. Without urgency or scarcity, people tend to put off decisions. And let's face it, procrastination rarely leads to a sale.

The problem isn't just what's written; it's the mindset behind it. Writing an email that appeals only to logic assumes your reader is ready to buy, but most people aren't. They need to feel something first. They need to imagine how their life could change, see proof that others trust you, or fear they might miss out on something valuable. These aren't just tactics—they're basic human instincts. Ignore them, and your emails are just white noise in a crowded inbox.

Selling to the Heart, Not Just the Head

If you want your sales emails to convert, you've got to flip the script. Instead of listing features or trying to explain why your product makes sense, focus on how it makes people *feel*. Tap into emotions like excitement, relief, or even curiosity. When people feel something, they act. When they only think something, they hesitate.

The secret is to meet your readers where they are emotionally. This means using triggers like scarcity, urgency, social proof, and reciprocity in your messaging. These aren't gimmicks—they're rooted in how people make decisions. Scarcity tells your audience that time is running out, and they need to act now. Reciprocity makes them feel valued, which builds trust. Social proof shows them they're not alone, that others trust you too. And urgency? That's the nudge that gets them to finally click the button.

But it's not just about using these principles—it's about tailoring them to the people on your list. Not everyone reads an email the same way. Some buyers respond to excitement and energy, while others need logic and reassurance. Some want to see what everyone else is doing, and others just need a deadline breathing down their neck. To write effective emails, know the buyer types. Speak directly to each.

The shift isn't complicated, but it requires intention. You're not just writing to sell a product. You're writing to connect, inspire, and move your reader to action. When you do it right, your emails won't feel like sales pitches—they'll feel like exactly what your reader has been waiting for.

6 Best Practices for Writing Emails That Convert

Writing a sales email that converts isn't about using fancy words or bombarding your readers with everything you can think of. It's about understanding what makes people tick, connecting on an emotional level, and guiding them to take the next step. Think of your email like a conversation—it should feel natural, engaging, and purposeful. These best practices will help you. They will let you use persuasion and buyer psychology. You'll craft emails that inspire action, not just sit in inboxes.

Practice 1. Leverage Scarcity to Create Demand

Scarcity works because people hate the idea of missing out. When something feels limited—whether it's time, availability, or access—it suddenly becomes more valuable. It's why limited-edition sneakers sell out in minutes and why restaurants with "only 10 seats left" fill up faster.

In your emails, scarcity can take many forms. Maybe it's a product with only a few units remaining, or perhaps it's a bonus offer that disappears after midnight. The key is to make your audience feel like they need to act quickly, or they'll miss their chance. For example, instead of saying, "We're offering a discount," say, "There are only 5 spots left at this price." Specificity amplifies the effect.

But here's the thing—scarcity only works if it's authentic. If your audience catches on that your "limited offer" isn't actually limited, you'll lose trust faster than you gained their attention. Be honest about your constraints, and use scarcity strategically to highlight real limitations.

Practice 2. Introduce Urgency to Inspire Action

Urgency gets people moving. When you add a ticking clock to your offer, you create momentum. Without it, people tend to procrastinate. They think, "I'll deal with this later," and later often turns into never.

One of the simplest ways to create urgency is by adding a deadline. Instead of saying, "Order now," say, "Order before midnight tonight to claim your discount." Deadlines give your audience a reason to act immediately. Pair them with visuals, like countdown timers, to make the time limit feel tangible.

But urgency doesn't have to be about time. It can also be about opportunity. Phrases like, "Secure your spot before they're gone," or, "Be one of the first to access this exclusive offer," tap into the same sense of urgency. Just like with scarcity, make sure your urgency feels real. If your deadline passes but your offer is still live, you'll train your audience to ignore your emails.

Practice 3. Showcase Social Proof to Build Trust

People look to others for guidance when they're unsure. Social proof is why restaurants with a long line out the door seem more appealing, or why you read reviews before buying something online. It's reassurance that someone else has already tested the waters.

Social proof works beautifully in sales emails. Use testimonials, success stories, or numbers to show how others have benefited from your offer. Instead of saying, "This course can help you grow your business," say, "Over 2,000 entrepreneurs have used this course to double their income."" Numbers are powerful because they make your claims feel grounded in reality.

Don't have testimonials yet? Borrow credibility by showcasing awards, partnerships, or mentions in reputable publications. Even phrases like, "As featured in Forbes," can make your offer feel more trustworthy. The goal is to show your audience that they're not taking a leap of faith—they're following a proven path.

Practice 4. Use Reciprocity to Build Goodwill

Reciprocity is simple: when you give something valuable, people feel inclined to give something back. It's why free samples work in grocery stores and why a thoughtful gift can turn a skeptic into a loyal customer.

In your emails, reciprocity could mean offering a free guide, checklist, or resource that genuinely helps your audience. The key is to make sure it's directly tied to your paid offer. If you're selling a course on writing better emails, your free gift might be a downloadable email template. It's a small taste of the value they'll get if they decide to buy.

What's counterintuitive here is that giving away something for free can actually increase your sales. Some might worry that people will just take the freebie and leave, but that's not usually the case. When your free content solves a real problem, people are more likely to think, "If this is free, imagine what I'll get when I pay."

Practice 5. Leverage the 4 Types of Buyers

Not everyone on your list thinks the same way. Some people decide quickly based on emotion, while others need all the facts before they commit. Recognizing these differences and tailoring your emails accordingly can make all the difference.

- **Spontaneous buyers** respond to excitement and energy. Use words like "amazing," "instant," or "can't-miss." Create urgency by emphasizing fast results or limited availability.

- **Methodical buyers**, on the other hand, want logic and details. Spell out the benefits clearly, include data or case studies, and reassure them that their decision is a sound one.

- **Social proof buyers** care about what others think. Highlight testimonials, reviews, and community stats to make them feel like they're part of something bigger.

- **Deadline-driven buyers**, as the name suggests, need a deadline to take action. Use phrases like, "This deal disappears at midnight," or, "Last chance to join us before the doors close."

The more you understand your audience, the more effective your emails will be. Tailor your tone, content, and persuasion techniques to meet them where they are.

Practice 6. Focus on a Single Call-to-Action

One of the fastest ways to derail your email is by overwhelming your readers with options. Multiple CTAs confuse people. Should they read the blog? Check out your product? Watch the video? When the choice isn't clear, people often make no choice at all.

Instead, every email you send should have one clear goal. If you want them to click a button, make it obvious. Remove distractions, and repeat your call-to-action in different ways throughout the email. For example, start with, "Click here to grab your spot," and end with, "Don't miss out—reserve your spot now." Consistency keeps the focus where it belongs.

A single CTA doesn't mean your email has to be boring. Use engaging language, build excitement, and make the next step feel irresistible. But remember, when you give readers too many paths, they'll get lost. Guide them to the one action that matters most.

Practical Exercise: Craft a High-Converting Email

Crafting an email that converts doesn't have to feel like guesswork. Follow this step-by-step guide to write a persuasive email tailored to your audience and designed to inspire action.

Step 1. Pick Your Target Buyer

Start by choosing one buyer type: Spontaneous, Methodical, Social Proof, or Deadline-Driven. Think about how this buyer makes decisions and what motivates them. Spontaneous buyers love excitement and quick wins. Methodical buyers need details and reassurance. Social proof buyers want to see that others trust you. Deadline-driven buyers are motivated by time-sensitive offers.

Ask yourself:

- What does this buyer care about most?

- What emotions will drive their decision-making?

- What objections might they have, and how can you address them?

Step 2. Write a Subject Line

Create a subject line that hooks your reader instantly. Use one persuasion principle—urgency, scarcity, social proof, or reciprocity—to capture attention. For example:

- Urgency: "Only 24 Hours Left to Secure Your Spot"

- Scarcity: "5 Spots Remaining—Act Fast"

- Social Proof: "Join Over 10,000 Happy Customers Today"

- Reciprocity: "Your Free Guide Is Waiting—Grab It Now"

Keep it short and compelling. If you're unsure, imagine your subject line competing with dozens of others in your reader's inbox. Which one would you click?

Step 3. Draft the Opening Sentence

Your first sentence sets the tone. Start with an emotional hook that makes your reader stop and pay attention. Paint a picture, ask a question, or make a bold promise. For example:

- "Imagine waking up tomorrow with more time, freedom, and clarity."

- "What's stopping you from achieving the results you deserve?"

- "The secret to doubling your productivity isn't what you

think."

Make it about them—not you. Speak to their desires, fears, or challenges.

Step 4. Incorporate a Persuasion Principle

Choose one persuasion principle and weave it into the body of your email. If you're using scarcity, you might write:

- "This opportunity won't last—there are only 3 spots left, and they're filling up fast."

If you're using social proof, you could say:

- "Over 5,000 entrepreneurs have already transformed their businesses with this program—now it's your turn."

Focus on one clear message. Avoid cramming multiple principles into a single email, as it can dilute your message.

Step 5. Add a Clear Call-to-Action

End your email with a single, direct call-to-action (CTA). Tell your reader exactly what to do next. Examples:

- "Click here to register now and secure your spot."

- "Download your free guide today and start seeing results."

- "Sign up before midnight to claim your exclusive bonus."

Make your CTA easy to spot—bold it, use a button, or repeat it at the beginning and end of your email.

Key Takeaways:

- Sales emails that convert rely on psychological principles like scarcity, urgency, social proof, and reciprocity to drive action.

- Tailoring your emails to different buyer types ensures your message resonates with their unique decision-making styles.

- Keeping emails focused, emotional, and clear—with a single, compelling call-to-action—is the key to maximizing conversions.

14

How to Use Evergreen Deadlines on Autopilot

D eadlines have a way of making us move. We've all felt it—that ticking clock that pushes us to act before it's too late. Jack Born, the creator of Deadline Funnel, learned this lesson firsthand in the early days of his entrepreneurial journey.

After leaving corporate America, Jack built a platform. It connected healthcare companies with nurses. It wasn't fancy—just a $70 script he found online—but it worked. One day, he decided to cut off access to his site, announcing a hard deadline. What happened next was a revelation. In just 24 hours, $27,000 in sales poured in. That single moment showed him the power of a deadline to turn hesitation into action.

But Jack didn't stop there. He spent years learning marketing from experts like Perry Marshall. He honed his understanding of funnels and conversions. He began to see a gap in the tools marketers had available. While deadlines worked, they were often messy to implement or, worse, felt fake and manipulative. Jack wanted something better. He wanted a system that could create a real urgency. It should be personalized for each customer, without compromising integrity.

That vision led to Deadline Funnel—a tool designed to automate authentic deadlines across devices. No resetting timers. No shady tactics. Just genuine urgency that motivates people to act.[8]

In this chapter, you'll discover how evergreen deadlines, powered by automation, can transform your sales process. They're more than just a timer. They're a system for creating trust, building urgency, and giving every subscriber a reason to pay attention. Done right, they don't just boost sales—they set the stage for long-term engagement and respect.

The Problem of Fake Urgency

When I first started experimenting with software Deadline Funnel, I wasn't sure what to expect. I'd run campaigns before with fixed deadlines, but I always had this nagging issue. People would miss the deadline, email me later, and ask if they could still get the deal. The truth was, the page was still live, and they could still buy. I'd tell myself it was easier this way—why say no to more sales? But deep down, I knew I was training my audience not to trust my deadlines.

Then one day, someone emailed me with a story that stuck. They had been juggling a busy week and missed the deadline. They reached out, hoping for an exception. For once, I didn't cave. The offer was closed, and the page was gone. I told them I'd announce the next deal when the time came. To my surprise, their response wasn't frustration. It was respect. They thanked me for being clear and fair.

That was the moment I realized what evergreen deadlines could do. They're not about tricking your audience. They're about creating structure, building trust, and teaching people to value your offers. Done right, they bring urgency and fairness together in a way that works for everyone.

The Power of Evergreen Automated Deadlines

Deadlines are one of the most effective tools for driving action, but only when they're real. Evergreen automated deadlines take this power to the next level. They combine urgency with personalization. This creates a system that works for you and your audience. Let's explore how these deadlines can transform your sales process, build trust, and keep your offers top of mind.

Legitimate Deadlines Build Trust

Deadlines lose their power if they aren't enforced. Automation brings structure and reliability, ensuring deadlines are consistent and fair. When subscribers know the offer disappears when the clock hits zero, they start paying attention. It's not about pressuring them; it's about being clear and dependable. People respect businesses that stick to their word. Trust is built one decision at a time, and when your deadlines are real, your audience starts to trust your process.

One effective way to enforce this trust is through a "sorry" page for expired offers. Instead of leaving the sales page accessible, redirect visitors to a page that acknowledges the deadline has passed. This simple step sends a strong message: you mean what you say. It's not about shutting people out; it's about reinforcing that your deadlines are genuine. Over time, your audience learns to act promptly, knowing your offers aren't just empty promises.

Evergreen Deadlines Personalize Urgency

Traditional deadlines often apply to everyone at once, which can feel arbitrary. Evergreen deadlines change the game by tailoring urgency to each subscriber's actions. This personalization ensures that every subscriber has a fair and relevant experience. It doesn't matter if they engage today or six months from now; their timeline starts when they do. This creates a sense of individual attention while maintaining consistency across your campaigns.

Imagine a subscriber opens an email on Wednesday, clicks the link, and sees a deadline that ends Saturday. Someone else clicks the same email days later and gets their own three-day deadline. Both experiences feel immediate and relevant because the deadlines adjust to the subscriber's journey. It's like being offered the best seat in the house, no matter when you arrive. This personalization not only drives action but also builds goodwill by making every subscriber feel seen.

Automation Enhances Scalability

Running a business means wearing many hats, and manually managing deadlines shouldn't be one of them. Automation allows you to set up deadlines once and let the system do the work. Tools like Deadline Funnel work with your existing platforms. They create a hands-off process that generates sales without constant oversight. It's like planting seeds in the background while you focus on growing other parts of your business.

Automated systems don't just save time—they create opportunities. Imagine an email sequence you set up months ago continuing to generate sales today. Someone new joins your list, clicks a link, and enters an automated sequence with their own personalized deadline. While you're working on a new project or spending time with family, your evergreen campaigns are still bringing in revenue. This scalability is a game-changer, especially for solopreneurs looking to maximize their impact.

Simplified Fixed Campaigns Still Deliver Results

Fixed campaigns are a great way to dip your toes into the power of deadlines. They're straightforward and effective, requiring only two pages: one for the sales offer and another for when the deadline has passed. Add a countdown timer to the sales page, and you've created instant urgency. It's simple, but simplicity doesn't mean it's ineffective. A clear, time-sensitive offer grabs attention and drives conversions.

For example, a weeklong campaign with a fixed deadline can generate a surge of interest and sales. Subscribers know they have until Friday at midnight to act, and the ticking clock keeps the urgency front and center. Once the deadline passes, the sales page redirects to a generic "sorry" page. This simple setup is easy to execute and still gives your audience a clear reason to act.

Enhanced Engagement with Triggered Broadcasts

Broadcast emails paired with triggered deadlines can inject urgency into real-time communication. By adding a tag when a subscriber clicks a link, you can automatically drop them into a personalized campaign. It's a seamless way to create urgency without overwhelming your entire audience. Instead of blasting everyone with a one-size-fits-all message, you're targeting the people most likely to act.

Imagine sending a broadcast email for a flash sale and including a link that activates a three-day deadline for anyone who clicks. This approach creates excitement while maintaining relevance. Subscribers who aren't interested can ignore the email, while those who click are rewarded with a timely, personalized offer. It's urgency with precision, giving you better results without alienating your audience.

Simplicity Beats Complexity

It's easy to get caught up in complex strategies, but sometimes the simplest solutions deliver the best results. Using basic fixed campaigns or a generic "sorry" page can have a big impact without overloading your workflow. These setups don't need much tech knowledge or setup time. So, they are accessible to any marketer.

A simple campaign might involve setting up a fixed deadline, adding a countdown timer, and redirecting to a single "sorry" page. This approach respects your audience's time while showing them that deadlines matter. As you grow more comfortable, you can layer in advanced features like evergreen campaigns. But even if you stick with the basics, you'll see how a little urgency can go a long way in boosting your sales and building trust.

Deadlines drive action. Without them, people hesitate, overthink, and move on. An automated deadline funnel lets you create real urgency without manually tracking every subscriber's journey. Follow these steps to set up your first evergreen automated deadline.

Practical Exercise: Create Your First Deadline Funnel

Step 1: Choose Your Offer

Pick a product or service you want to promote. This could be:

- An online course

- A paid workshop

- A membership trial

- A limited-time coaching package

Make sure it's something valuable and relevant to your audience. The more aligned your offer is with their needs, the more effective your deadline funnel will be.

Step 2: Set a Deadline

Decide how long someone should have to claim your offer. Three days is a good starting point. It's long enough for people to make a decision but short enough to create urgency.

Think about your audience's behavior. If they typically take their time, a five-day deadline might work better. If they're more impulsive, 48 hours could be the sweet spot. The goal is to find the right balance—just enough time to consider, not enough time to procrastinate.

Step 3: Create Two Pages

Your deadline funnel needs two key pages:

- **Landing Page**: This is where you sell the offer. Include a clear headline, compelling copy, and a countdown timer that matches your deadline. If the timer says three days, it should actually expire in three days for each visitor.

- **"Sorry" Page**: Once the deadline passes, this is what people see instead of the offer. Keep it friendly. A simple message like "This offer has expired, but stay tuned for future opportunities" works well. You could also direct them to another relevant offer or a waitlist.

Step 4: Set Up Automation

The magic of an evergreen deadline funnel is that it runs on autopilot. Here's how to set it up:

- In your email marketing platform, create a trigger. This could be when someone clicks a link in your email or opts into a freebie.

- Apply a tag to that subscriber, signaling that their personal deadline has started.

- Connect this tag to your deadline tool (such as Deadline Funnel or Countdown Hero). This ensures that each person gets their own unique countdown—whether they click today or two months from now.

Step 5: Test the System

Don't assume it works. Test everything.

- Click the email link yourself and make sure the countdown appears on the landing page.

- Wait until the deadline expires and check if the system correctly redirects you to the "sorry" page.

- Try opening the page in a different browser or device to see if the countdown stays accurate.

Once you've verified everything is working, your deadline funnel is ready to go. Every new subscriber will enter their own countdown, creating urgency without you lifting a finger.

Key Takeaways

- Legitimate deadlines build trust and teach your audience to take your offers seriously.

- Evergreen deadlines personalize urgency, creating a fair and relevant experience for each subscriber.

- Starting with simple fixed campaigns can deliver powerful results and set the foundation for more advanced automation.

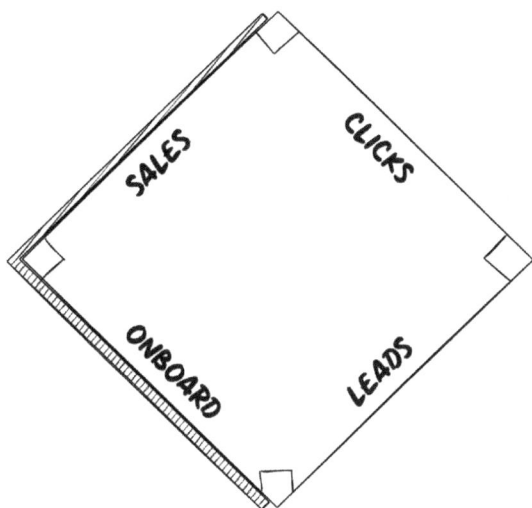

Home Base:
Welcoming
Customers

15

Home Base: Welcoming New Customers

T he Washington Post knew they had a problem. Subscribers were signing up, but too many weren't sticking around. They had a great product—a world-class news platform—but something wasn't clicking. Then, they made a simple but powerful shift: they started paying attention to how they welcomed new subscribers. They didn't just send a generic "thanks for signing up" email. They made a personalized onboarding journey. It walked readers through what they'd just signed up for. It helped them find stories that mattered to them. It showed them how to get the most from their subscription.

So, what were the results? Subscribers who went through their new onboarding sequence stayed longer, engaged more, and were far more likely to renew. By simply focusing on how they welcomed people, they transformed their business.[9]

Welcoming new customers might not seem like the most exciting part of running a business, but it's where everything begins. The first few interactions set the tone for the entire relationship. Get it wrong, and customers could disappear before they've even scratched the surface of what you offer. Get it right, and you're building a foundation for loyalty, trust, and long-term revenue.

This chapter is all about that foundation. It's about the power of onboarding. It can help you retain customers and guide them to your higher-value offers. You don't need flashy tactics or hard sells. You just need to meet people where they are, show them the value you bring, and help them take the next step.

When you welcome people well, they don't just stay—they thrive. And so does your business.

The Wrong Way to Welcome: Common Pitfalls

Welcoming a new customer should feel like opening the door to a warm, inviting space. But, businesses often make mistakes. Customers feel overwhelmed, confused, or second-guessing their purchase. These missteps can turn an exciting first impression into a missed opportunity for connection and trust.

Drowning in Details

Some businesses make the mistake of overloading new customers with too much information all at once. They send long emails packed with features, benefits, and every possible thing a customer *might* want to know. The result? Overwhelm. Instead of feeling excited, customers feel like they've been handed a manual they don't have time to read. They disengage before they even begin.

Leaving Them Lost

Others don't give clear next steps. A customer signs up, but then what? They're left guessing how to get started or what to do next. When people feel confused, they lose momentum. And once that momentum is gone, it's hard to get it back.

Coming On Too Strong

There's also the temptation to push for an upgrade right out of the gate. Customers barely have time to explore what they've bought before they're hit with an upsell. It feels like a bait-and-switch, and instead of saying yes, they're more likely to back away.

Skipping the Human Touch

Finally, too many businesses forget the power of a simple, personal connection. A generic "thank you for your purchase" doesn't make anyone feel special. Without a personal touch, customers don't feel valued, and the relationship starts off cold.

Why These Mistakes Drive Customers Away

A chaotic onboarding experience makes customers doubt their choice. They lose confidence in your business. Instead of building trust, these mistakes create barriers that push people away. A rocky start can turn even the best product or service into a forgettable experience.

Information Overload Equals Disengagement

When people feel overwhelmed, they check out. It's human nature. Customers who don't know where to focus their attention are more likely to hit delete on your emails—or worse, unsubscribe altogether.

Confusion Breeds Regret

Without clear guidance, customers can start to second-guess their purchase. If they don't see quick wins or understand the next step, they might start thinking they made the wrong choice.

Pushiness Kills Trust

Trying to sell an upgrade too soon makes people question your intentions. Are you there to help them or just squeeze more money out of them? This kind of approach erodes trust and makes future offers harder to sell.

Missed Chances to Connect

When businesses skip the opportunity to create a personal connection, they lose out on the chance to build loyalty. A warm, thoughtful welcome can make all the difference in how customers perceive you—and whether they stick around.

These pitfalls might seem small, but they can have a massive impact on your bottom line. The good news? Each one is completely avoidable.

Home Base: Welcoming New Customers

The first impression isn't just about saying hello—it's about showing your new customer they made the right choice. A warm, supportive welcome creates an experience where people feel seen, valued, and confident they're in the right place. Onboarding isn't just a process; it's the start of a relationship.

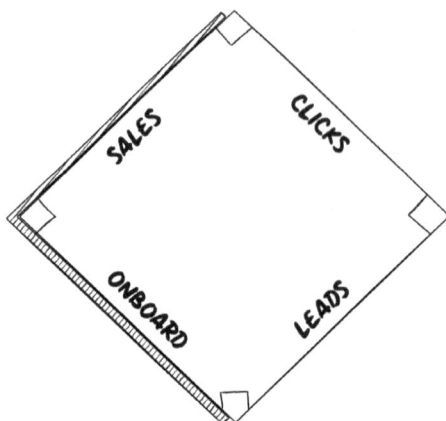

When you approach onboarding with value and care, you turn curiosity into commitment. Instead of overwhelming your customers, guide them step by step. Help them see quick wins and real results early on. It's not about flashy promises; it's about delivering on what you said you would.

The best onboarding experiences feel like a conversation, not a transaction. They answer questions before they're asked and encourage customers to take the next step, one at a time. With the right foundation, you'll build a connection that grows stronger over time.

Build Relationships That Last: The Cornerstones of Onboarding

Onboarding is your chance to turn first-time buyers into lifelong customers. It's about creating a journey that feels personal, helpful, and exciting. When you make people feel welcome and guide them toward success, they're more likely to stick around and explore what else you have to offer.

Here's how to craft an onboarding experience that leaves customers feeling confident, valued, and ready to take the next step.

Create a Warm Welcome

The start of any relationship sets the tone for everything that follows. When someone makes a purchase, they're already leaning into trust—your job is to meet them there with a genuine welcome. A personal thank-you message or video isn't just polite; it shows that you care about their decision and value their presence.

Imagine receiving a short, friendly video that says, "Thank you for joining us! We're thrilled to have you here, and we can't wait to help you achieve your goals." This simple touch creates a human connection, making the customer feel more than just a number. It also lowers their guard and encourages engagement from the start.

The welcome is also your chance to reinforce their choice. Highlight what they've just gained and give them a glimpse of what's next. For instance, you might say, "You've just unlocked access to [specific benefit]. Up next, we'll show you how to [quick win or result they'll achieve]." This shifts the focus from "what they spent" to "what they'll gain," building excitement and trust.

Map Out a Success Path

Every journey is easier when you know where you're going. Onboarding should act like a GPS for your customers, providing step-by-step guidance to ensure they get the most out of what they've purchased. People don't want to figure things out on their own—they want you to lead the way.

Start by identifying the key actions customers need to take to see results. If it's software, that might mean completing their first setup. If it's coaching, it might mean watching an intro video or scheduling their first session. Lay these steps out clearly, so there's no guess-work.

Quick wins are the secret sauce here. When customers see results early, even small ones, it boosts their confidence and motivates them to keep going. For example, a fitness app might guide users to log their first workout or track their first meal. These small victories create a sense of progress and reinforce the value of your product.

Deliver Value Before Asking for More

Think of onboarding as a chance to serve, not sell. Help customers use their purchases fully. Then, introduce upgrades or extra offers. When you lead with value, people naturally want more.

Send helpful resources like guides, tutorials, or tips tailored to where they are in their journey. For instance, a course creator might send an email with, "Here's how to set yourself up for success in Module 1." These resources should be practical, actionable, and designed to make their experience better.

When customers feel like they're gaining insights and seeing results, they're far more open to hearing about what else you offer. You're not just pitching them—you're solving their problems and showing how your next product or service can help them even further.

Time Your Offers Strategically

Timing is everything. An upgrade offer feels helpful when it's pre-sented at the right moment but intrusive when it's pushed too soon. The key is to understand when your customer is ready to hear it.

Milestones are a great indicator. If a customer completes their on-boarding process or reaches a specific goal, that's the perfect time to suggest an upgrade. For example, "You've completed the beginner level—ready to take your skills to the next stage?" This approach feels natural because it's tied to their progress.

Behavioral triggers also work wonders. If a customer is highly engaged—opening your emails, using your product, or exploring features—they're ready for more. A well-timed email like, "We noticed you've been loving [feature]. Here's how you can unlock even more benefits," feels personalized and relevant.

Show Social Proof

People trust people. Sharing success stories, testimonials, or case studies is very effective. It builds credibility and inspires confidence in your offers. When customers see others benefiting from an upgrade, it's easier for them to imagine themselves doing the same.

Highlight stories that align with your customer's goals. For instance, "Sarah used [your product] to save 10 hours a week—here's how she did it." Or, "This upgrade helped John double his results in half the time." Specific results create a vivid picture of what's possible and help customers see the value of taking that next step.

Social proof isn't just about numbers; it's about emotion. When people feel like others have succeeded, they're inspired to follow suit. Pair testimonials with results that matter most to your audience, and you'll create a compelling case for your ascension offers.

By combining these principles—welcoming customers warmly, guiding them clearly, delivering value, timing offers, and showing proof—you go beyond just onboarding. You're building a relationship that lasts.

Practical Exercise: Map Your Onboarding Strategy

Before diving into the step-by-step creation of an onboarding email sequence in the next chapter, take a moment to zoom out and assess your current onboarding approach (or, if you don't have one yet, outline your ideal strategy). The goal is to create a structured, welcoming journey that keeps customers engaged from the moment they sign up.

Step 1: Define Your Onboarding Goal

Every onboarding experience should have a clear purpose. What do you want your new customers to feel, know, and do within their first few interactions?

- Are you helping them understand how to use a product or service?

- Do you want them to take a key action (e.g., log in, watch a video, complete a task)?

- Is your main focus engagement, retention, or guiding them toward an ascension offer?

Write a one-sentence statement that defines the goal of your onboarding experience. Example:
"My onboarding process will guide new customers to their first quick win within 48 hours, ensuring they feel confident and excited about their purchase."

Step 2: Identify Key Milestones

Map out three to five key milestones that a new customer should hit in their first few days or weeks. These should be meaningful moments that show progress and reinforce their decision to join.

Example milestones:

1. **Welcome & Orientation:** They receive a warm, personal welcome message explaining what to expect.

2. **First Action Taken:** They log in, explore their dashboard, or watch an introductory video.

3. **Quick Win Achieved:** They complete a small, meaningful task that shows immediate value.

4. **Engagement & Support:** They interact with a community, support resource, or bonus content.

5. **Next Steps Introduced:** They receive guidance on how to continue and possibly an introduction to an ascension offer.

Now, write down your own milestones and ensure they provide a smooth and rewarding journey.

Step 3: Audit Your First Impression

Imagine you're a brand-new customer experiencing your business for the first time. Ask yourself:

- Does my current onboarding process feel simple and welcoming, or overwhelming and confusing?

- Is the first communication clear, engaging, and helpful?

- Are there unnecessary gaps where new customers might feel lost or disengaged?

- Am I balancing education with encouragement, ensuring they feel valued and excited?

If you already have an onboarding process, make a list of what's working well and what could be improved. If you don't have one yet, jot down a few must-have elements you want to include.

Step 4: Plan for Long-Term Engagement

Onboarding doesn't end after the first email. How will you keep new customers engaged beyond the first few days? Consider strategies like:

- A welcome sequence that gradually introduces them to different features or benefits.

- A weekly check-in or progress email to encourage engagement.

- Invitations to join a community or interact with your brand in a meaningful way.

Write down one way you will keep customers engaged after their initial onboarding experience.

Step 5: Outline Your Next Steps

Based on what you've just mapped out, list three simple actions you can take to improve (or build) your onboarding process.

For example:

1. Rewrite my welcome message to feel more personal and inviting.

2. Create a "quick win" activity that helps customers see immediate value.

3. Plan a follow-up email at the one-week mark to encourage continued engagement.

By taking the time to map out your onboarding strategy now, you'll be in a great position to craft your email sequence in the next chapter. A thoughtful welcome experience doesn't just retain customers—it turns them into loyal, engaged fans of your business.

Key Takeaways

- A thoughtful onboarding process creates trust and confidence, setting the stage for a strong relationship with your customers.

- Guiding customers to quick wins early in their journey builds momentum and keeps them engaged.

- Well-timed and value-driven ascension offers naturally lead customers to explore more of what you offer, increasing loyalty and lifetime value.

16

How to Create an Onboarding Sequence

Y ou've just launched your membership site. Signups are rolling in, but you're worried. Will these new members stick around? Will they truly engage with your product? Enter Wistia, a video hosting platform that faced these exact challenges.

Wistia's story is a testament to the power of a well-crafted onboarding email sequence. They took a bold step, redesigning their emails with a laser focus on guiding new users towards key actions and product features. The result was a staggering 350% increase in conversions from their new onboarding emails.

But what made Wistia's approach so effective? They didn't just send a series of random emails. They created a funnel, carefully moving prospects through the stages of awareness. Each email had a purpose, from stoking the ego with vanity metrics to showcasing ease of use and tying the product directly to business growth.

Wistia's success wasn't just about the emails themselves. They also revamped their product-led onboarding strategy. They invested in user research and feedback. So, they tailored the onboarding experience to what users actually needed, not what the team thought they needed.

This approach paid off. Activation levels jumped by 15-20% when they introduced a product tour video at the start of the onboarding process. It's a great example of how to use email and in-product experiences. Together, they can create a powerful onboarding tool.[10]

As we create onboarding email sequences to turn new signups into happy, long-term customers, keep Wistia's story in mind. It's not just about sending emails. It's about crafting a journey that guides your members to success, one carefully planned step at a time.

Welcome to the Whirlpool: Why Most Onboarding Fails

A lot of memberships kick off with the same cookie-cutter approach: a single, generic welcome email. It's polite, sure. It might even be enthusiastic. But it's as impersonal as a generic handshake at a crowded party. There's no mention of the member's unique goals or why they joined in the first place. It's like being handed a user manual when you really need a tour guide.

From there, it often gets worse. The member is hit with a fire-hose of information—links, resources, features, and calls to action—dumped all at once. It's overwhelming.

Where do they start?

What's the most important thing to focus on?

Without clear direction, many members simply freeze. Instead of feeling excited, they feel like they just walked into a library where all the books have been thrown into one giant pile.

Then, there's the emotional void. Sure, the welcome email might list some benefits, but it doesn't speak to the deeper reasons why people join. People don't just sign up for information; they want connection, inspiration, and a sense of belonging.

Yet, these onboarding efforts often skip over the chance to say, "Hey, you're part of something special now." Instead, new members are left to figure things out alone, like the new kid on the first day of school who doesn't know where to sit at lunch.

Without personalization, guidance, or emotional connection, onboarding turns into a missed opportunity. Members don't just lose momentum—they lose interest. And once that spark is gone, it's hard to get it back.

Turning First Impressions Into Lifelong Connections

Onboarding isn't just about logistics; it's about building a relationship. It's the difference between handing someone a map and walking alongside them on the journey. This isn't a transaction where you check a box and move on—it's the start of something meaningful.

Instead of throwing everything at your new members all at once, think of onboarding as a slow reveal. Introduce one key element at a time. Let them savor the experience. Progress should feel natural and manageable, not like cramming for a final exam.

The most effective onboarding creates a pathway to success that's as clear as a well-lit runway. It aligns with why members signed up in the first place. What do they want to achieve? What small wins will help them believe they're on the right track? When you show them exactly where they're headed, they'll trust that they're in the right place.

But logic alone doesn't create loyalty. People stick around when they feel connected. They want to know they're not just another name in the system—they're part of something bigger. When your onboarding makes people feel seen, supported, and valued, they're not just members; they're fans.

Every message you send should have a purpose. Stay focused. Stay consistent. Make each step feel like progress, and tie it to something tangible.

When members can see results—no matter how small—they'll stay engaged and invested. Onboarding done right is like planting seeds. With care and intention, those seeds grow into a thriving, loyal community.

The 9-Day Email Onboarding Blueprint

Onboarding isn't about bombarding new members with content—it's about building a journey they'll want to take. Each email in your onboarding sequence must be a small, meaningful step. It should reinforce their decision to join and show them how to succeed. This approach isn't just about delivering information; it's about creating momentum, trust, and excitement. Here's how each day of the sequence plays a key role in turning members into engaged, loyal participants.

Day 1: Welcome and Getting Started

The first email sets the tone. A warm welcome makes members feel like they've arrived at the right place. Share login details and direct them to the "Get Started" page to avoid confusion. End with an invitation to explore the community—a subtle way of saying, "You belong here."

Day 2: Setting Goals

This email is about helping members clarify their "why." Ask them to share their goals and remind them of the core membership features that align with those goals. Encourage them to take their first step by focusing on one recommended piece of content. This sets the stage for progress without overwhelm.

Day 3: Call to Community

The community is where relationships grow. This email emphasizes the importance of connection and collaboration. Highlight how the community can provide accountability, feedback, and support. Then, invite members to introduce themselves—it's a small step with a big impact.

Day 4: Highlight a Core Feature

By Day 4, members are ready to discover the tools that will help them succeed. Introduce a key feature, like a roadmap or course library, and explain its purpose. Show how it simplifies their journey by giving them a clear focus.

Day 5: Check-In

A personal check-in shows members they're not just a number. Ask how they're finding the membership so far. This isn't just about troubleshooting—it's about creating a moment of connection and demonstrating that you're invested in their success.

Day 6: Calendar of Events

Introduce the rhythm of your membership with a reminder about live calls or events. Share links to your calendar and explain how they can participate, even if they can't attend live. Highlight the value of these events in creating a deeper connection to the membership.

Day 7: Highlight Additional Features

This is the moment to reveal another layer of value. This email reminds members of perks they may not have explored. They include accountability partners, planning calls, and a resource library. Tie the feature to the outcomes they're working toward.

Day 8: Proof of Success

Stories inspire action. Share testimonials from members who've achieved results using your resources. Highlight their wins to help others visualize their own success. Encourage members to connect with the community for inspiration and support.

Day 9: Request for Testimonials

This email invites members to reflect on their journey so far. A request for testimonials isn't just about gathering praise—it's about reinforcing the value of the membership in the member's mind. Offer easy ways for them to share their thoughts, making it a win-win for everyone.

Each of these emails serves as a step in a larger narrative. They help members find clarity, connection, and confidence. They turn an overwhelming start into a structured, meaningful experience.

Practical Exercise: Design Your Onboarding Email Sequence

Step 1: Define the Purpose of Your Sequence

Write down the primary goal of your onboarding sequence. Is it to make members feel welcome? Help them see quick wins? Foster a sense of belonging? Be clear and specific about the emotional and practical outcomes you want your members to experience.

Step 2: Identify Key Moments in the Member Journey

Consider the key points in your membership. Members need clarity, connection, or encouragement at these times. Write a list of these moments, such as the first login, setting goals, engaging in the community, or attending their first live event.

Step 3: Choose Themes for Your Emails

For each key moment, assign a theme that aligns with the member's needs at that stage. Use the 9-day sequence from this chapter as inspiration, or create your own. Keep the themes focused on one clear message per email.

Step 4: Map Out Your Sequence

Create a simple outline of your email sequence. For each email, jot down:

- The theme or purpose of the email.

- The key message or takeaway you want the member to understand.

- The action you want the member to take after reading the email.

Step 5: Prioritize Emotional Connection

Look back at your sequence and ask yourself: Are there moments where members feel seen and valued? Add elements that build an emotional connection. Use personal stories, encouragement, and invitations to engage with others.

Step 6: Write Your First Email

Draft your welcome email. Focus on creating a warm, inviting tone. Include login details, a link to a "Get Started" page, and an invitation to explore the community. Be clear, concise, and action-oriented.

Step 7: Test and Refine

After drafting your emails, read through them as if you're a brand-new member. Ask yourself:

- Does this email feel welcoming and helpful?

- Is the action step clear and easy to follow?

- Does it align with the emotional and practical goals of the sequence? Make adjustments based on your answers.

Step 8: Get Feedback

If you already have a membership, ask a few trusted members to review your onboarding sequence. Gather their feedback on what feels helpful or missing, and use it to improve your emails.

These steps will create a powerful onboarding sequence. It will drive long-term engagement and satisfaction.

Key Takeaways

- A well-crafted onboarding email sequence is essential for creating happy, engaged members and improving retention rates.

- Most onboarding sequences fail because they overwhelm new members, lack emotional connection, and don't provide clear guidance.

- An effective onboarding sequence builds trust through progressive engagement, aligns with members' goals, and fosters a sense of belonging.

17

How to Create an Upgrade Sequence

You've just sold a flashlight for $18. Not bad, right? But what if that single sale could turn into a $20 million windfall? Well, that's exactly what Trey Lewellen, a master of internet marketing, pulled off with his tactical flashlight funnel.

Trey's story is a masterclass in the art of the upsell. He didn't just sell a flashlight; he created a value ladder that customers couldn't resist climbing. Here's how it worked:

1. The hook: A tactical flashlight for $18

2. The quick upsell: Rechargeable batteries

3. The long-term commitment: 1-year or 3-year warranty

Simple, right? But here's the kicker - this straightforward approach generated over $20 million in just six weeks. That's not just impressive; it's industry-shattering.

What made Trey's strategy so effective? It wasn't just about selling more stuff. It was about offering continuous value at each step. Customers didn't feel like they were being sold to; they felt like they were being taken care of.[11]

Think about it. You buy a flashlight, and immediately you're offered batteries. It makes sense, right? You need batteries for your new flashlight. Then comes the warranty offer. Again, it's a logical next step. You've invested in this great flashlight, so why not protect it?

This is the essence of a well-crafted upsell sequence. It's not about pushing products; it's about anticipating needs and offering solutions. It's about creating a journey that feels natural and beneficial to the customer.

As we dive deeper into the world of upgrade offers in email sequences, keep Trey's flashlight funnel in mind. It's a shining example of how a well-thought-out upsell strategy can turn a simple product into a multi-million dollar success story.

Why Most Businesses Miss Out on Easy Wins

Most businesses treat a customer's purchase like the end of the story. The sale is made, the payment is processed, and they send a simple, bare-bones email with login details or access information. That's it. No fanfare, no follow-up, no opportunity for the customer to do anything more.

Here's the problem: they're leaving money on the table.

There will always be a percentage of buyers who would buy more from you if you made it available to them. But instead of striking while the iron's hot, most businesses ignore this golden moment.

When someone has just made a purchase, they're in an emotional state of satisfaction and trust. They've already said "yes" to you once, which makes them far more likely to say "yes" again. Psychologists call this the "yes ladder." But if all you do is deliver the product and walk away, you're slamming the door on that opportunity.

Imagine a customer buying a car. The salesperson hands over the keys but never offers upgrades like better tires, a protection plan, or even a fancy air freshener. It seems absurd, right? But in the digital world, that's what many businesses are doing.

It's not about being pushy. It's about meeting people where they are. There's a small window when buyers are primed for more, and it's your job to offer them something that adds value to their journey. Otherwise, you're not just missing out on additional revenue—you're missing a chance to deepen the relationship.

This isn't just a missed opportunity for your business; it's a missed opportunity for your customer. They trusted you enough to buy from you. Why wouldn't you offer them more of what they need to succeed?

Make Every Purchase Feel Like the Start of Something Bigger

The moment someone buys from you, they've taken a leap of faith. They've trusted you to help solve a problem or achieve a goal. What they need now isn't just access to what they purchased—they need validation. They need to feel like they made the right choice, and they want to know what comes next.

This is where most businesses drop the ball. They stop the conversation. But you can do something different.

Start by reinforcing the value of their purchase. Congratulate them on their decision. Make it clear they've taken a step toward solving their problem or achieving their goal. This simple acknowledgment goes a long way in creating trust and excitement.

Then, present an upgrade that makes their journey even smoother. Show them your offer isn't just another product. It's a tool that helps them use what they've already bought—faster, easier, or with better results.

For example, let's say someone just bought a meal-planning guide. Instead of just sending the guide, offer a membership. It would provide pre-filled, weekly shopping lists and recipes, based on their preferences. You're not just giving them more; you're removing friction and saving them time.

The key is to make the upgrade feel like a natural extension of their purchase. Position it as the next logical step, the thing that takes their results to the next level. Use language that connects the dots for them:

- "Now that you've got the Profit Playbook, the Growth Academy will help you put it into action faster."

- "You've taken the first step—let's make it even easier for you to succeed."

- "Why stop here? Let's build on your momentum and get you results sooner."

Your upgrade offer should feel like you're holding out your hand, inviting them to go further with you. It's not about selling—it's about serving. When done right, it deepens the relationship and ensures your customers feel supported every step of the way.

How to Create Your 4-Day Upgrade Email Sequence

Let me use a practical example from one of my upgrade sequences. When someone purchases one of my $17 Profit Playbooks, they've already taken a significant first step. They've made an investment, said "yes" to their goals, and trusted me to guide them. This is the perfect moment for me to invite them deeper into the journey. The key is to not just deliver what they purchased but to show them how they can take their progress even further. That's where the upgrade to one of my $45/month membership comes in.

The academy isn't just "more content." It's a continuation of the value they've already invested in. The Profit Playbook is a helpful resource. But, the academy gives access to every other playbook, coaching, community, and tools. They will help you implement faster and easier. Over the course of four days, this upgrade sequence does one thing: It invites them to go further. Each email focuses on a specific theme to move them from a single purchase to becoming a monthly member. Let's break it down.

Day 1: Congratulations and Next Step

The first email in the sequence is all about celebrating the customer's decision. They've purchased the $17 Profit Playbook, and that's a big deal. This email focuses on validating their choice, reminding them that they've already taken an important step toward their goals. People like to feel that they're on the right path, and this email reinforces that belief.

It's also the perfect moment to let them know that there's an even bigger opportunity ahead. While the Profit Playbook is valuable on its own, the academy offers so much more. Framing this as a VIP, limited-time offer adds urgency. It makes it a special opportunity. The goal is to plant the seed that joining the academy is the natural next step for amplifying their success.

This email should feel encouraging and exciting. The tone is optimistic, focusing on their potential and showing them that they've already started their journey. By the end of the email, they should feel validated, motivated, and curious about what's waiting for them inside the academy.

Day 2: The Power of a Community of Raving Fans

The second email shifts gears to inspiration and education. The goal is to reveal the "secret" to a successful online business. It is to create a community of raving fans who will buy their ideas before they are even created. This is a counterintuitive idea for many, which makes it compelling. It challenges the idea that success needs a huge audience, complex strategies, or endless hustle.

This email taps into the power of storytelling. By sharing examples of others who have succeeded through the Market Your Message Academy, you're painting a vivid picture of what's possible. These stories make the idea of joining the academy feel more tangible and relatable. It's not just theory—it's a proven system that's already working for people just like them.

The tone here should be inspiring and aspirational. It's about helping them see the bigger picture and showing them what's possible when they take the next step. This email isn't about pushing—it's about inviting them to dream bigger and showing them that the academy can help make those dreams a reality.

Day 3: Addressing Questions and Concerns

By day three, some customers will still be on the fence. This email is designed to tackle their hesitations head-on. Common concerns—like whether they have enough time, whether the academy is right for them, or whether it's too complex—are natural. Instead of ignoring these doubts, this email addresses them directly and provides reassurance.

Each question is an opportunity to build trust. For example, if they're worried about time, you can emphasize that the academy is self-paced and designed to fit into their schedule. If they're concerned about tech, you can highlight how the academy focuses on simple, low-tech strategies. Every answer should help remove a potential barrier to their decision.

The tone is empathetic and supportive. This email shows that you understand their concerns and genuinely want to help them succeed. It's not about convincing them. It's about making them feel confident that joining the academy is a smart, low-risk decision that aligns with their goals.

Day 4: Last Chance to Join

The final day is all about urgency. By now, the customer knows the value of the academy and how it can help them. This is their last opportunity to take advantage of the 72-hour VIP offer, and this email reminds them of that fact.

The morning email sets the stage. It emphasizes that time is running out and reminds them of everything they'll gain by joining the academy. The tone is direct but still encouraging. It's about helping them see that this is a chance to avoid wasted time and effort by learning a proven system that works.

The evening email is the final push. It simplifies the message, cutting straight to the core of why they should act now. It highlights the academy's benefits, clears up any doubts, and stresses that the offer ends when time runs out. The tone here is urgent and firm, making it clear that this is their last chance to say "yes."

By the end of day four, every customer will have had multiple opportunities to take the next step. Whether they join or not, they'll walk away feeling supported, respected, and empowered to make the best decision for their goals.

Practical Exercise: Create Your Own 4-Day Upgrade Sequence

Use this exercise to craft a compelling upgrade sequence for your own product or service. Outline each email using the steps below. Your sequence must engage, educate, and convert customers into recurring members.

Step 1: Define the Upgrade Offer

Before diving into the emails, clarify what you're offering as the upgrade. Write down:

- The core value of the upgrade (e.g., "Access to a library of tools and resources to simplify implementation").

- Why this upgrade complements the original purchase.

- The exclusive nature of the offer (e.g., limited-time, VIP access).

- The pricing and any risk-reduction (e.g., cancel anytime, low-cost trial).

Step 2: Draft Your Day 1 Email

Theme: *Congratulations and Next Step*

- Write a warm opening that celebrates the customer's decision.

- Reassure them that they've made a smart choice with their initial purchase.

- Transition into introducing the upgrade as a natural next step.

- Highlight key benefits of the upgrade in bullet points or a short, persuasive paragraph.

- End with an exclusive, time-sensitive offer and a clear call to action (CTA).

Example AI Prompt: "Write a 3-paragraph email congratulating your customers on their purchase and inviting them to explore an exclusive upgrade. Use a positive, encouraging tone."

Step 3: Draft Your Day 2 Email

Theme: *The Power of What's Possible*

- Start by reinforcing the value of their initial purchase.

- Introduce the "big idea" behind the upgrade—why it's a game-changer.

- Use a story or example of someone who has succeeded with the upgrade.

- Explain how this upgrade simplifies or accelerates their results.

- Close with an invitation to learn more and remind them of the time-sensitive nature of the offer.

Example AI Prompt: "Write a 4-paragraph email sharing a compelling success story that ties into your product upgrade. Highlight the unique benefits of upgrading and invite them to take the next step."

Step 4: Draft Your Day 3 Email

Theme: *Overcoming Objections*

- Open by acknowledging that they might have questions or concerns.

- List 3–5 common objections, and write clear, reassuring answers for each.

- Include examples or proof to back up your answers (e.g., testimonials, screenshots).

- End by emphasizing the low-risk nature of the offer and the urgency of the deadline.

Example AI Prompt: "Write a 5-paragraph email that directly addresses potential objections to your product upgrade. Make it empathetic and solution-focused."

Step 5: Draft Your Day 4 Emails

Morning Email Theme: *Urgency and Recap*

- Open by reminding them that time is running out.

- Recap the key benefits of the upgrade.

- Frame the decision as a way to avoid wasted time or effort.

- End with a direct CTA to join before the offer expires.

Evening Email Theme: *Final Push*

- Use a bold opening like, "This is it..." to create a sense of finality.

- Reiterate the core message: why this upgrade matters and how it helps them succeed.

- Add a brief "you have nothing to lose" reassurance (e.g., cancel anytime).

- Close with a firm, time-sensitive CTA.

Example AI Prompt: "Write two emails for the final day of your upgrade offer. The first should create urgency, while the second should be direct and final, leaving no doubt about the next step."

Key Takeaways

- Customers are most likely to upgrade immediately after their initial purchase, so timing is crucial.

- Validate your customer's decision before introducing an upgrade to build trust and reinforce their confidence.

- Focus on how the upgrade helps them implement their initial purchase faster, easier, or with better results.

18

Real-Life Example of the Diamond Map in Action

Some things make more sense when you see them in action. That's exactly what this chapter is about.

You know the theory behind the Diamond Map. It shows how to turn a casual interest into a paying customer. You do this with click magnets, story-based emails, and automated sales sequences. But theory only takes you so far. What does this look like when it's actually running? How does it flow from step to step? What happens after someone clicks?

This chapter walks you through a real-life example, step by step. Imagine setting this up once and then being able to trigger sales whenever you want, with just a single email. That's the power of this system.

For this example, let's assume you already have a product or course to sell. You've got your email sales sequence dialed in. You're using an evergreen timer like Deadline Funnel. The pieces are in place. Now, it's time to light the match and watch it run.

Step One: Choose a Click Magnet

Everything starts with a click. Before someone enters your sales sequence, they need a reason to engage. That's where a **click magnet** comes in. A click magnet is anything that delivers free value while nudging people toward your offer. It could be a checklist, a template, a spreadsheet, or a short training video. The key is that it solves a small but meaningful problem—something so useful that your audience wants it immediately.

If you're stuck on what to create, keep it simple. One of the fastest click magnets to produce is a **5-10 minute training video**. You don't need slides or fancy editing. Just teach something practical, record it, and upload it to a basic landing page. Beneath the video, place a button that says, *Download the PDF* or *Grab the Template*. This button leads straight to your opt-in. No fluff, no distractions.

For this example, the click magnet is the **Lazy Workshop PDF**, a simple guide on how to make money teaching on Zoom. It's specific, actionable, and directly tied to the offer that comes later. That's another crucial piece—your click magnet should naturally lead into your paid product. If the click magnet solves a small part of the problem, your course or product should provide the full solution.

The beauty of this approach is that it works in almost any niche. In fitness, business, personal development, or writing, you can create a valuable resource in minutes. The key is to focus on something that's **instantly helpful** and leaves them wanting more. When done right, your click magnet won't just attract clicks—it will attract **the right people**, those who are already interested in what you have to offer.

Step Two: Write a Story-Based Email

A click magnet on its own won't do much. People need a reason to care, a reason to take action. That's where a **story-based email** comes in. Stories grab attention, stir curiosity, and make an idea stick. Instead of saying, *Hey, here's a free PDF*, you tell a story that naturally leads to your click magnet, making it feel like the next logical step.

The story doesn't have to be dramatic. It just needs to connect. For example, to promote the **Lazy Workshop PDF,** you could tell a story about how traditional free webinars used to be a goldmine for selling courses. But over time, attendance dropped, engagement dipped, and conversions tanked. That left a big question: *How do I still get people to show up and buy?* The answer? **Charge for the workshop.** Even a $25 price tag changes the entire dynamic. People show up, they engage, and they take action. That's the lesson, and the natural transition is: *Want to see how I do it? Grab my Lazy Workshop PDF here.*

You can use almost any story as long as the **lesson ties directly to the offer.** Maybe it's about your first paid workshop and how surprised you were when people actually signed up. Maybe it's about a failed attempt at free webinars that forced you to pivot. The structure stays the same: **Hook → Problem → Lesson → Action Step.**

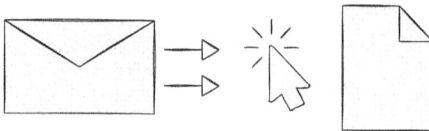

When the email lands in inboxes, some people will skim, some will delete, and some will read all the way through. The ones who click? Those are the ones raising their hands.

They're signaling interest.

That's why this step is so powerful—it doesn't just drive clicks, it filters out **the right** clicks, setting up your sales sequence for success.

Step Three: Tag Clickers and Automate the Sales Sequence

Clicks mean interest, but without a system in place, those clicks go nowhere. This is where automation comes in. Instead of manually tracking who engages with your emails, you let your email marketing software do the heavy lifting.

The goal is simple: **anyone who clicks the link to grab your click magnet gets tagged and automatically added to your sales sequence.**

Most email platforms make this easy. In Kajabi, for example, you can create an automation that says, *If someone clicks this link, add the tag "2B: CLICK: Lazy Workshop PDF."*

This tag acts like a backstage pass—it tells your system, *Hey, this person is interested in this topic. They're a potential buyer.*

From there, another automation kicks in, moving them straight into the sales sequence. No manual work. No delays. The moment they click, they're on the path to your offer.

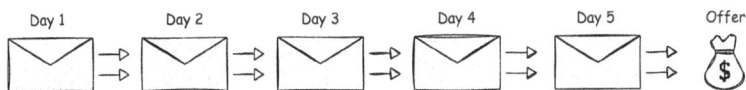

Think of it like a theme park. Everyone enters through the front gate (your email list), but not everyone rides the same attractions. Some people stop at the first ride and leave. Others keep moving deeper into the park, exploring what's next. The tag acts like a wristband that guides them to the next ride—the **Lazy Workshop Playbook sales sequence.**

Without tagging, you're guessing. You're sending the same emails to everyone, hoping something sticks. With tagging, you're only selling to people who've **already expressed interest.**

This means higher engagement, better conversions, and fewer un-subscribes. More importantly, you can repeat this. Send another story-based email and feed more people into your automated funnel. Once the system is set up, it works **forever.**

Step Four: Send the Story-Based Email and Monitor the Automation

With everything set up, it's time to send the email. This is where the system starts working in real-time. You hit send, and within minutes, people begin opening, reading, and clicking. Some will grab the click magnet immediately. Others will save it for later. Either way, **your automation is waiting,** ready to tag and move them into the sales sequence.

The key here is to watch what happens. Check your email stats. Are people opening the email? Are they clicking the link? If clicks are low, maybe the subject line needs tweaking. If opens are solid but clicks are weak, maybe the story isn't compelling enough. Every email you send is **data**—a chance to learn what resonates with your audience.

Once everything looks good, you can **repeat the process** anytime you want. The best part? You're not just selling once. Every new email is another opportunity to pull more people into your sales sequence.

Most of the time, you won't send just one email and call it a day. In-stead, you might send **three to five story-based emails over a week,** each leading to the same click magnet. This keeps your audience engaged and continuously feeds your funnel.

If the automation is working correctly, you'll see sales coming in—sometimes immediately, sometimes days later. That's the beauty of an evergreen system. **Emails sent today can generate sales weeks from now.** And because everything runs on autopilot, your only real job is to write compelling emails and let the system do the rest.

Step Five: Upgrade Buyers to a Recurring Offer

A $17 sale is great, but it's just the beginning. The real magic happens when a buyer moves from a **one-time purchase to a recurring subscription.** That's why the next step in the automation is to **tag buyers and introduce them to the upgrade sequence.**

In this example, anyone who buys the Lazy Workshop Playbook for $17 is added to an upgrade sequence. It invites them to join Growth Academy for $45/month.

The logic is simple: if they found the Playbook valuable, they'll likely want access to even more resources. And, instead of selling them something new, you position the membership as an upgrade that unlocks everything.

This sequence runs for about five days, giving buyers time to explore their purchase before presenting the next step. It's not a hard sell. It's an **invitation**—a natural extension of what they've already bought.

The emails highlight the benefits: more Playbooks, ongoing support, deeper training. The idea isn't to convince them to spend more money. It's to show them that they're **already in the right place—now they just need full access.**

Only the most engaged buyers will take this next step, but that's a good thing. These are the people who are most likely to stick around long-term. Some will upgrade immediately.

Others will wait and come back later. But once this sequence is in place, every new Playbook buyer gets the same opportunity—**on autopilot.** Over time, this turns what started as a simple $17 sale into a steady stream of **recurring revenue.**

Here's a diagram of the entire process from start to finish:

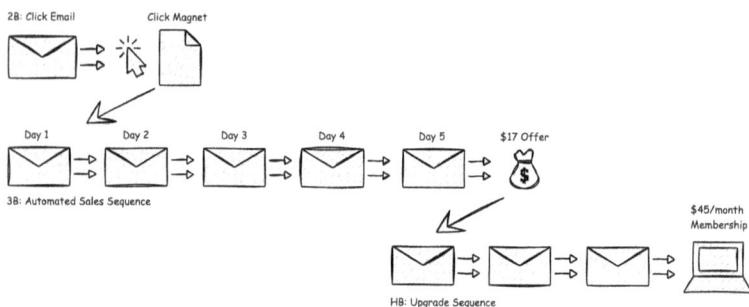

Bonus: Making Sales Long After You've Promoted Your Click Magnet

One of the most overlooked benefits of this system is that **it keeps working long after you hit send.** Most people think of email pro-motions as temporary—once the email is sent, the results stop. But when you set up automations correctly, old emails can still generate new sales **weeks or even months later.**

Here's how it works: Some subscribers don't check their email every day. Others skim but don't take action right away. But at some point—maybe a week later, maybe a month—they go back, open an old email, and **click the link to grab your click magnet.** Your automation runs in the background. So, that simple action triggers the entire sales sequence, as if they clicked the day you sent it.

This means your past emails are still doing their job, quietly moving people through your funnel even while you're focused on something else. The result? **Sales trickle in long after your initial promotion ends.** You're no longer stuck in the cycle of constantly launching and chasing new leads. Instead, your system keeps working in the background, making every email you send **a long-term asset instead of a one-time event.**

This is the power of evergreen automation. Once it's set up, every click has value—whether it happens today, next week, or three months from now.

Pro Tip #1: Use Naming Conventions to Stay Organized

Once you have a handful of sales sequences running, things can get messy fast. Without a clear system for naming your emails, tags, and automations, you'll waste time searching for things, duplicating work, or—worst of all—**breaking a sequence without realizing it.** That's why naming conventions matter.

A good naming system makes everything easy to track. For example, here's how the **Lazy Workshop** funnel is labeled internally:

- Tags – 2B: CLICK: Lazy Workshop PDF

- Broadcast Emails – 2B: CLICK: Story Email 1

- Automated Sales Sequence – 3B: OFFER: Lazy Workshop Playbook

- Upgrade Sequence – HB: UPGRADE: Academy

Each label serves a purpose. The numbers indicate where each step falls in the process. The keywords (CLICK, OFFER, UPGRADE) tell you exactly what the tag or email is doing. With a system like this, you can **instantly search and find what you need**, even when you have **10-15 sales sequences running at once.**

Without this kind of structure, it's easy to lose track. Imagine trying to remember which email links to which sequence, or worse—accidentally sending the wrong offer to the wrong group. A few minutes spent organizing things now **saves hours later** and keeps your funnel running smoothly, no matter how big it gets.

Pro Tip #2: Create a Click Magnet Database

Most people treat click magnets like one-and-done assets. They create a freebie, promote it for a while, and then move on to the next thing. That's a mistake. A well-crafted click magnet can be **reused, repurposed, and recycled**—but only if you keep track of them. That's where a **Click Magnet Database** comes in.

This is simply a running list of every click magnet you've ever created. You can store it in **Notion, a Google Sheet, or even a basic document.** The goal is to create a catalog of click magnets that are ready to go whenever you need them. A good database includes:

- **The name of the click magnet** (e.g., *Lazy Workshop PDF*)

- **The format** (PDF, video, checklist, template, etc.)

- **The last time it was used** (so you know when to bring it back)

- **The corresponding sales sequence** (so you can reconnect it to an offer)

This becomes incredibly useful as your business grows. Instead of scrambling to create something new every time you want to run a promotion, you **just pull from the database.** If a click magnet performed well in the past, it will likely perform well again—especially since new people are always joining your list.

Think of it like a playlist. You don't have to create a brand-new song every time you want to share music. Sometimes, you just bring back an old favorite. A Click Magnet Database ensures that your best lead magnets never go to waste—and lets you **run sales sequences on demand with minimal effort.**

Seeing the Diamond Map in action makes one thing clear—it's not about chasing sales. It's about **building a system** that brings in sales automatically. Once the foundation is in place, you're no longer relying on constant promotions, exhausting launches, or hoping the right people find your offer. Instead, you create **a repeatable process** that turns interest into income anytime you need it.

It all starts with a simple **click magnet**—something valuable enough to get people to take action. Then, a **story-based email** brings it to life, making the offer feel natural instead of forced. With **tagging and automation**, every click triggers the next step, guiding people deeper into your sales sequence. The result? A system that keeps working **long after you've moved on to the next project.**

This isn't just about making sales—it's about **making smart sales.** Instead of blasting promotions to your entire list, you're speaking directly to the people who have already raised their hands. And by layering in an **upgrade sequence**, you're turning small purchases into long-term customers.

The beauty of this approach? It only gets easier. The more click magnets, story emails, and sequences you create, the more **flexibility**

and control you have over your revenue. At any time, you can open your **Click Magnet Database**, send an email, and watch the system go to work. Once you see it in action, you'll never go back to the old way of selling again.

Key Takeaways

- **Automation turns one-time promotions into ongoing sales**—by tagging clickers and triggering a sales sequence, you can generate revenue long after an email is sent.

- **Story-based emails make click magnets more effective**—a compelling story creates an emotional connection, making people more likely to engage and take action.

- **A click magnet database saves time and increases sales**—recycling proven click magnets allows you to quickly launch promotions without constantly creating new content.

19
The Power of Bunt Email Campaigns

E ver heard of a business that thrives on breaking its own rules? Sounds crazy, right? But some of the most successful strategies are the ones that flip the script. Let's take a closer look at a story that'll leave you rethinking everything you thought you knew about rules.

Picture a bustling deli in Ann Arbor, Michigan. The air is thick with the smell of fresh-baked bread and perfectly seasoned meats. Customers are laughing, sharing stories, and savoring meals that feel more like love letters than lunch. But there's something different here. Something you can't quite put your finger on.

This isn't your ordinary deli. This is Zingerman's.

At Zingerman's, rules are made to be broken—but not for the sake of chaos. Ari Weinzweig, the mind behind this $65-million-a-year empire, has one simple philosophy: break the rules to serve the customer. It's a radical idea, but it works like magic.

What does that look like? Imagine a server whipping up an off-menu masterpiece because a customer couldn't decide. Or a staffer sneaking in early to help someone who's craving their famous sandwich before opening hours. There's even a workaround for their no-reservations policy—if you've got a special request, they'll find a way to make it happen. Every broken rule feels like a little gift wrapped in care and topped with a bow of "just for you."

It's the kind of service that makes customers come back, time and time again. And the numbers don't lie—Zingerman's is thriving. But this isn't reckless behavior. It's calculated risk-taking. It's smart, intentional, and always customer-focused. It's about bending the rules, not breaking trust.[12]

This chapter is about finding your own version of Zingerman's secret sauce. When does it make sense to color outside the lines? How do you strike the balance between structure and spontaneity? And, most importantly, how can some rule-breaking spark huge growth and loyalty? Let's get to it.

The Power of Bunt Email Campaigns

We've talked a lot about nurturing relationships with your audience before making the ask. Most of the time, a structured customer journey map is best. It builds trust and guides people to become loyal customers. But sometimes, just like in baseball, you need to switch up your strategy and bunt. A bunt isn't about hitting a home run. It's about making a strategic move to advance the runner—or in our case, drive short-term results without abandoning the bigger picture.

Bunt email campaigns are a little like that strategic play in baseball. They're not meant to replace your regular email cadence. They're not something you do all the time. But when used sparingly and intentionally—maybe once or twice in a 90-day cycle—they can be powerful. A bunt campaign is direct, focused, and unapologetically aimed at selling. It's not about nurturing or storytelling; it's about delivering a timely, compelling offer that most of your audience can't resist.

The key to a successful bunt campaign is timing and purpose. These campaigns work best when your offer appeals to your list. It should align with their interests or solve a common problem. For example, you might run a flash sale on a product that's been performing well or launch a limited-time offer on a new service. The idea isn't to abandon your relationship-building strategy but to temporarily step outside the lines for a focused push.

Bunt campaigns thrive on urgency. A countdown timer, limited availability, or even an exclusive bonus can drive the action you're looking for. But here's the catch: you can't overuse them. If you're constantly pitching, you'll train your audience to only respond to discounts or feel like they're being spammed. The power of a bunt campaign lies in its rarity. It's the unexpected element that grabs attention and sparks action.

Think of bunt campaigns as a tool in your marketing toolbox. They aren't your strategy's foundation. But, they're useful for a quick win without derailing your long-term goals. Used wisely, bunt email campaigns can be a game-changer—helping you score while keeping your audience engaged and excited.

Bunt Campaign 1. The 4-Day Flash Sale Campaign

Flash sale campaigns are the quintessential example of a bunt campaign. Think of Black Friday sales—a perfect storm of scarcity, urgency, and excitement. They only happen once a year, they're short-lived, and they offer big discounts. All those elements combined make these campaigns both thrilling and profitable. For the majority of the year, I'd recommend leading with value and segmenting your audience through click magnets. But with a flash sale like Black Friday, it's all hands on deck. This is the kind of offer that everyone on your list should know about.

Flash sales don't have to be limited to Black Friday, though. You can sprinkle them throughout the year—perhaps for a spring sale, a back-to-school campaign, or a Valentine's Day special. The key is to limit these to once per quarter, or no more than four times a year. Why? Because you don't want to train your audience to expect sales every week. If they know another sale is always just around the corner, they'll lose the urgency to act. The rarity is what makes flash sales special.

Here's how I structure a 4-day flash sale campaign. Over the course of four days, I send one email per day, each targeted to a specific type of buyer. Spontaneous buyers will likely jump on the first email, which emphasizes the excitement and exclusivity of the offer. Methodical buyers will need more details, so the second email focuses on the features and benefits. Social proof buyers will respond to testimonials and case studies, which I include in the third email. Finally, deadline-driven buyers will act after the last email. It highlights the ticking clock and reminds them they're running out of time.

Bunt Campaign 2. Book or Product Launches

Launches are another powerful bunt campaign strategy. New books and limited-time product launches aim to create buzz and urgency. Book launches, in particular, are a great example. When I launch a book, I devote an entire week to it, with every email pointing directly to the buy button. This isn't the time for click magnets or complex segmentation. It's about putting the spotlight on your latest work and making sure your entire audience knows about it.

That doesn't mean the emails are purely sales pitches. In fact, I weave in stories, principles from the book, and lessons that give readers a taste of the value they'll get when they buy. For instance, I might share a personal story that inspired a chapter or reveal a surprising stat that ties into the book's main theme. This approach creates excitement and helps readers connect with the content before buying.

You can apply the same strategy to product launches. Whether it's a seasonal enrollment period for a course or the debut of a new service, the idea is the same: focus your emails on the launch for a short period of time, then return to your regular nurturing cadence. By limiting the window of opportunity, you create a sense of urgency that drives action.

Bunt Campaign 3. Live Virtual Paid Workshops

Live virtual paid workshops are a fast and simple way to generate cash and test interest in a topic. What I love most about this strategy is that it's lean. You don't need months of planning or production. In fact, you can sell the workshop before you even create it. The process is simple: float an idea for a workshop in an email or on social media at the start of the week. Ask your audience to reply or comment if they're interested. If the feedback is positive, you're ready to move forward.

Once the topic is validated, set up an order form and start selling. Over the next four days, send one email each day inviting your list to sign up. The workshop typically takes place on Saturday, and it's hosted via Zoom. The pricing is accessible—usually between $25 and $100 per ticket. If 100 people sign up for a $25 workshop, that's $2,500 in revenue for a single week of effort. And because the topic is based on audience interest, attendance is almost guaranteed.

I usually run these workshops about four times a year. They're a great way to engage your audience, provide value, and create a sense of community. Plus, they're a fantastic tool for validating new ideas.

If a workshop is particularly successful, it could even serve as the foundation for a larger course or product down the line.

Bunt Campaign 4. In-Person Events

For my annual two-day in-person event, direct selling is key. These events are a significant investment for attendees, so I start promoting tickets six to nine months in advance. My pricing strategy is simple. I start with a super early bird rate of about $200. I set a clear deadline for when the price will go up. Each month, the price goes up by $100 until it reaches the regular ticket price of $500. This tiered pricing creates urgency and rewards early decision-makers.

To sell tickets, I don't rely on click campaigns. Instead, I send direct sales emails to the entire list. These emails show why the event matters. They include testimonials from past attendees and stress the perks of buying tickets early. Spreading the campaign over several months lets me maintain momentum. It consistently fills seats without overwhelming my audience.

In-person events are a unique opportunity to connect with your audience on a deeper level. They build trust, foster community, and create memories that last long after the event ends. But, like any bunt campaign, their success depends on clear communication, strong offers, and a well-timed strategy.

Bunt campaigns are powerful. They drive short-term results without losing the big picture. They generate excitement, create urgency, and provide a change of pace from your regular email cadence. But the key is balance. Use them sparingly—no more than a few times a year—and focus on leading with value the rest of the time. When done right, these campaigns can boost revenue, build engagement, and keep your audience eager for what's next.

Practical Exercise: Plan and Execute Your First Bunt Campaign

This exercise will guide you step-by-step in creating and launching a successful bunt campaign. By the end of it, you'll have a clear plan, a compelling offer, and a ready-to-execute strategy for driving short-term results.

Step 1: Clarify Your Goal

Start by asking yourself a simple question: What do you want to achieve with this campaign? Maybe it's selling a specific number of products, driving ticket sales for an event, or generating buzz for a new book launch. Write your goal down in one sentence.

For example: *"I want to sell 50 tickets to my virtual workshop by the end of this week."*

Step 2: Choose Your Campaign Type

Decide which type of bunt campaign fits your goal. Is it a flash sale, a product launch, or a workshop promotion? The choice should align with your audience's interests and the urgency of your offer.

For instance, if you're promoting a time-sensitive workshop, a live virtual paid workshop campaign might be your best fit. If you're launching a new product, focus on creating excitement around its debut.

Step 3: Build Your Offer

Your offer needs to be both valuable and time-sensitive. Think about what will grab your audience's attention and make them act quickly. This could be a special discount, a bonus add-on, or limited availability.

For example: *"I'll offer 25% off my course for the next four days, plus a bonus live Q&A session for anyone who buys during the campaign."*

Step 4: Write and Schedule Your Emails

Plan your email sequence with four focused messages. Each email should serve a specific purpose:

- **Day 1:** Create excitement. Announce the offer and emphasize its exclusivity.

- **Day 2:** Provide details. Highlight the benefits and features of your product or service.

- **Day 3:** Use social proof. Share testimonials, case studies, or success stories.

- **Day 4:** Push urgency. Remind readers the offer ends soon and urge them to act now.

Draft these emails in advance and schedule them to send automatically over the campaign's duration.

Step 5: Set Up Your Campaign

Prepare everything you'll need to execute the campaign seamlessly. This includes: a clear landing page or checkout process, countdown timers, and a ready email platform. Please check that all links work. Also, make sure your emails and ads have the same message.

Key Takeaways

- Strategic rule-breaking creates excitement and momentum when used sparingly

- Urgency and a clear offer are the backbone of any successful bunt campaign

- Balance direct sales with value-based emails to maintain trust with your list

20

Your 90-Day Action Plan

L earning is great. Action is better.

By now, you have everything you need to **monetize your email list** using the **Diamond Customer Journey Map.** But knowledge without execution leads nowhere. That's why this chapter is all about putting your strategy into motion—**step by step, week by week.**

A **90-day plan** gives you structure, momentum, and a clear finish line. Instead of feeling overwhelmed by what you've learned, use a simple, repeatable system. It will turn your list into a money-making machine.

The 13-Week Roadmap

This plan is broken down into **four phases**, each building on the last. In 90 days, you'll have an automated email marketing system. It will grow your list, nurture your subscribers, and generate sales on autopilot.

Phase 1: Build Your Foundation (Weeks 1-3)

- Define your **core message**—What problem do you solve? Who do you serve?

- Set up your **email platform** (if you haven't already).

- Create or refine your **lead magnet**—make it irresistible and directly tied to your offer.

- Design a **simple landing page** with a clear, compelling call to action.

Phase 2: Engage & Nurture (Weeks 4-6)

- Set up a **welcome email sequence**—this introduces new subscribers and sets expectations.

- Write and schedule **weekly story-based emails** that build connection and trust.

- Track open rates and click-through rates. Adjust your subject lines and email content based on engagement.

- Gather feedback—pay attention to replies and subscriber behavior.

Phase 3: Monetize & Automate (Weeks 7-10)

- Create and test a **Click Magnet Offer**—this is your entry-level paid product ($7-$27).

- Set up **automated tagging**—anyone who clicks on a key link gets segmented.

- Write and automate your **sales sequence**—5-7 emails that sell your offer naturally.

- Monitor conversions—tweak subject lines, email copy, or offers based on performance.

Phase 4: Scale & Optimize (Weeks 11-13)

- Launch a **simple upgrade sequence**—offer a higher-value

product or membership.

- Refine your **Diamond Customer Journey Map** based on real data.

- Build a **Click Magnet Database**—start repurposing old lead magnets for new promotions.

- Plan your next 90 days—what worked? What needs improvement? What's the next offer?

Take Action Now

You don't need to have everything perfect to get started. **Progress beats perfection every time.** If you take consistent action for 90 days, you'll do more than build an email list. You'll have a system that brings in leads, builds trust, and generates sales.

Your audience is waiting. **Start today.**

21

What's Next?

Y ou made it. You've learned the strategies, systems, and mindset shifts needed to monetize your list. Now, email marketing can be a powerful, predictable revenue stream. That's no small accomplishment.

If you're feeling a mix of excitement and uncertainty right now, that's completely normal. Implementing what you've learned will take some trial and error. Some emails will land perfectly, while others may fall flat. But here's the truth—**every misstep is just another step toward mastery.** The more you engage, test, and refine, the stronger your list (and your confidence) will become.

One thing is certain: **your voice matters.** Your unique insights, experiences, and perspective are valuable, and the people on your list need to hear from you. The strategies in this book weren't designed to box you in—they were built to help you create a system that feels natural and sustainable. **You already have everything you need to succeed.** The automation, segmentation, and storytelling techniques you learned here will help you. They will help you to:

- Overcome common hurdles

- Stand out in crowded inboxes

- And turn subscribers into lifelong customers.

As you move forward, **stay optimistic**. It's easy to get caught up in numbers—open rates, click-throughs, conversions—but don't lose sight of the real goal: **impact**. Your email list isn't just a collection of names; it's a community. Whether you're teaching, coaching, inspiring, or selling, every message you send has the power to make a difference.

To boost your learning and stay motivated, I recommend getting the Monetize Your List Companion Workbook.

It helps you apply these concepts step by step. It gives you a way to map your strategies, track your progress, and keep moving forward. Consider it your personal guide to building momentum and making email marketing work for you.

No more second-guessing. No more waiting for the perfect moment. **Your audience is out there, waiting to hear from you.** Now's the time to take action. Stay consistent, stay bold, and most of all—**keep showing up.** Your dream of making an impact is within reach, and this is just the beginning.

1. "Les Frenchies Travel: Case Study." *GetResponse*, GetResponse, https://www.getresponse.com/customers/les-frenchies-travel.

2. Gardiner, Kate. "The Story Behind 'The Furrow', the World's Oldest Content Marketing." *Contently*, 3 Oct. 2013, https://contently.com/2013/10/03/the-story-behind-the-furrow-2/.

3. Basilio, Chenell. "How Justin Welsh Built a $1.7M Solo Business in Just 3.5 Years." *Growth in Reverse*, 12 Dec. 2024, https://growthinreverse.com/justin-welsh/.

4. Banko, Allison. "Email Marketing: Clothing Retailer Lifts Average Open Rate 40% via Customer Segmentation Campaign." *MarketingSherpa*, 12 Sept. 2013, https://marketingsherpa.com/article/case-study/lift-average-open-rate-segmentation.

5. Madrigal, Alexis C. "Hey, I Need to Talk to You About This Brilliant Obama Email Scheme." *The Atlantic*, 29 Nov. 2012, https://www.theatlantic.com/technology/archive/2012/11/hey-i-need-to-talk-to-you-about-this-brilliant-obama-email-scheme/265725/.

6. "TechSoup Polska Case Study." *GetResponse*, GetResponse, https://www.getresponse.com/customers/techsoup.

7. "Coca-Cola: A Short History." *The Coca-Cola Company*, https://www.coca-colacompany.com/content/dam/company/us/en/about-us/history/coca-cola-a-short-history-125-years-booklet.pdf.

8. "Interview with Jack Born of Deadline Funnel." *MemberMouse*, 2 Apr. 2020, https://membermouse.com/podcast/jack-born-deadline-funnel/.

9. Iyer, Anjali. "Personalized Subscriber Onboarding Results in Higher Engagement, Retention for Washington Post." *Washington Post Engineering*, 30 June 2023, https://washpost.engineering/personalized-subscriber-onboarding-results-in-higher-engagement-retention-for-washington-post-d5e1450821b8.

10. Wiebe, Joanna. "We Did These 7 Things to a SaaS Onboarding Email Sequence, and It Tripled Paid Conversions." *Copyhackers*, 1 Aug. 2017, https://copyhackers.com/2017/08/saas-onboarding-email/.

11. "The Flashlight Campaign that Ignited Native Advertising." *Affiliate World Conferences*, https://affiliateworldconferences.com/blog/flashlight-campaign-ignited-native-advertising/.

12. Weinzweig, Ari. *Zingerman's Guide to Giving Great Service*. Hyperion, 2004.

www.ingramcontent.com/pod-product-compliance
Lightning Source LLC
Chambersburg PA
CBHW061024220326
41597CB00019BB/3405